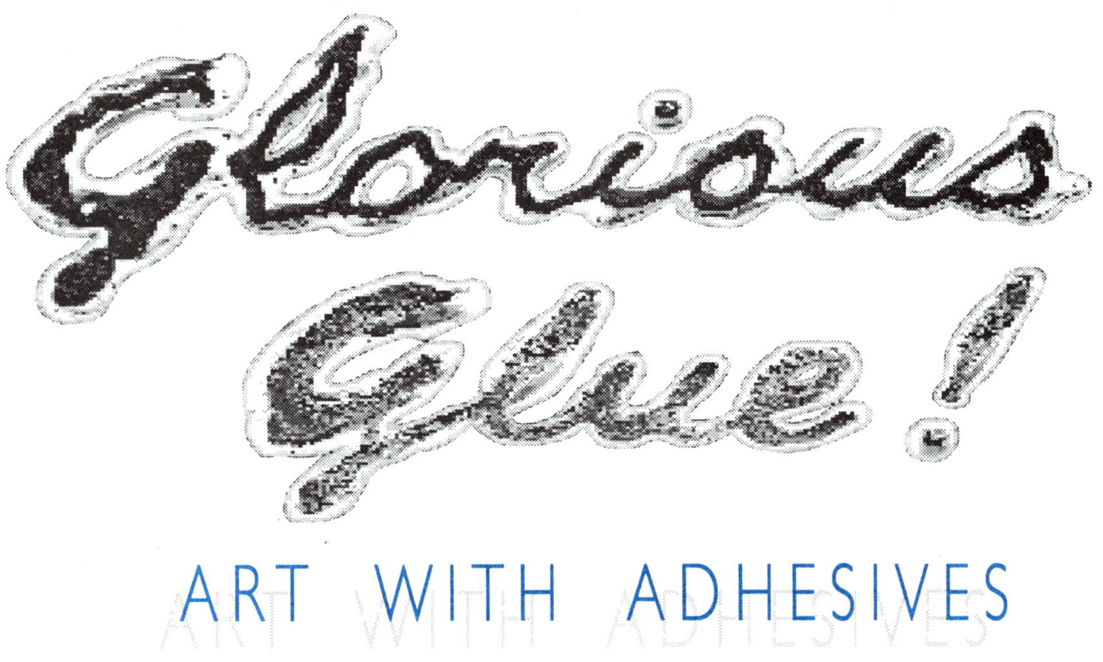

ART WITH ADHESIVES

Paula Guhin

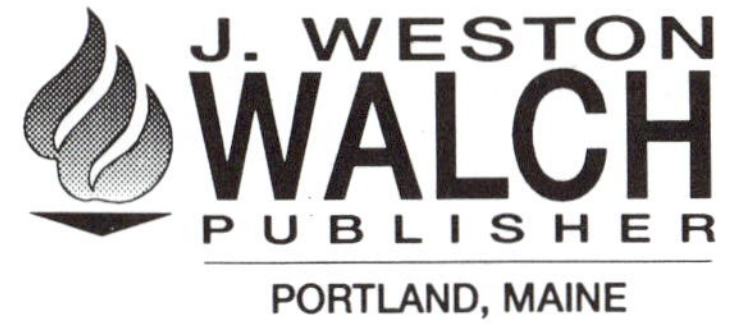

PORTLAND, MAINE

1 2 3 4 5 6 7 8 9 10

ISBN 0-8251-2690-8

J. Weston Walch, Publisher
P. O. Box 658 • Portland, Maine 04104-0658

Printed in the United States of America

Contents

Acknowledgment .... *v*

About the Author .... *vii*

Introduction .... *ix*

Supplies and Equipment .... *xi*

Chapter I. Catch the Sun, Feed the Birds 1

Chapter II. Raised Glue Designs and Relief Prints 3

Chapter III. Glue and Pastels—A Dynamic Duo 7

Chapter IV. Black Glue:
A Winner with Watercolors 11

Chapter V. Rubber Cement Resist—Remarkable! 15

Chapter VI. Glue Collage and Turpentine Resist 17

Chapter VII. Tip-Top Tissue and Crepe Paper Too 21

Chapter VIII. Recipes for Fun—Powder Prints, Paste Batik, and
More 25

Chapter IX. Marvelous Masks 33

Chapter X. String Things and Yarn Art 35

Chapter XI. Made Anew with Glue—Terrific Transformations .. 39

Conclusion *43*

Glossary *45*

Acknowledgment

Thanks to all of my stimulating students,
many of whom created the artwork pictured in this book.

About the Author

Paula Guhin is an art teacher at the junior and senior high levels in the Aberdeen, South Dakota, school system. A frequent contributor to a number of educational publications, she is a member of the National Art Education Association and has presented *Glorious Glue* at the NAEA Convention.

Introduction

Squish! Drip, squiggle, squirt! Have a grand time creating two- and three-dimensional works of art with adhesives as one of the main ingredients. Use squeeze bottles of the glutinous ooze to produce imaginative creations. Have fun with free-flowing, spontaneous lines that are curvy or angular or dotty.

Learn too how to incorporate shape, form, texture and color into great gluey artworks. Mix your media with watercolors, chalk pastels, markers, tissue and crepe paper and more. Experiment with rubber cement—it is supremely slimy stuff. Recycle discards into delightful designs. Giving trash new life as a work of art is fun and good for the environment too. Do papier-mâché the easy way: Make masks that are up close and personal. Also easy is a user-friendly method of batiking without wax. Use string and starch to form stimulating sculptures. Try printmaking and collage techniques as well. You'll find some holiday suggestions and even glue pretzels—they're for the birds!

There are easy, proven projects in this book appropriate for artists of all ages. For your convenience we've added skills ratings: easy, moderate, and advanced. Easy and moderate projects will be well within the grasp of middle-school students, while advanced projects may be best suited to high-school ages. We've also noted easy cleanup projects and projects that are perfect for partners.

To help you in evaluating completed works, we've included information upon which to base assessment. Finally, there is a helpful glossary of definitions at the end of the book.

If one of your artworks doesn't seem to turn out right, don't be disappointed or discouraged. Glue does not always go where you want it to. Accidents happen, and sometimes they can be incorporated into a successful design.

This sticky business is quite inexpensive, and we'll show you how to make some low-cost substitutions to save even more. There are recipes in Chapter VIII for some great homemade clay, putty, and other sticky stuff.

The art projects in this book are designed to help develop visual discrimination and to stimulate creativity. The guidelines should be freely interpreted in a nonrestrictive manner. Since each person brings her or his own skills and background to a project, each adventure in this book will provide a different experience for every artist.

Supplies and Equipment

- Alum
- Aluminum foil, heavy-duty
- Art gum eraser
- Birdseed
- Black construction paper
- Brayer (ink roller)
- Brushes
- Cardboard, poster board, or tagboard
- Clear glue
- Cloth rags
- Colored chalk pastels
- Colored inks
- Colored tissue papers
- Contact cement
- Containers
- Cornstarch and corn syrup
- Crayons
- Crepe paper

- Discarded mechanical objects
- Electric mixer
- Fixative or hair spray
- Flour
- Food coloring
- India ink
- Kitchen powders (cinnamon, cocoa, paprika, etc.)
- Lacquer thinner or turpentine
- Large balloons
- Liquid starch
- Magazines
- Markers, various sizes and colors
- Masking tape
- Measuring cup
- Mucilage
- Muslin fabric
- Newspapers
- Oil of wintergreen
- Paper towels
- Pencils
- Plaster of paris
- Pliers
- Powdered laundry detergent

- Rubber cement with brush applicator
- Sawdust
- Scissors
- Screwdrivers
- Sieve or screen
- Tempera or acrylic paints
- Thread
- Vinegar
- Wallpaper paste
- Water-base printing ink
- Watercolor paints
- Waxed paper
- Wheat paste powder
- White drawing paper, 9 × 12 or larger
- White glue, in a squeeze bottle
- Yarn or heavy string

Chapter I

Catch the Sun, Feed the Birds

• Light Catchers •

(PLATES 1–6)

Skills rating: Easy
An easy cleanup project

Squeezing out glue blobs is fun. A playful project with glue and markers is to make glue "stickies" or sun catchers, also called light catchers. They're translucent, pretty, and easy.

On a piece of waxed paper, form solid, filled-in glue shapes. Use either white or clear glue. Try to keep the shapes fairly small in size (several inches in diameter). You might try to form shapes that resemble something, but remember that glue has a way of spreading into something else entirely. Find the top of the shape and press the end of a piece of thread into it. Let it dry thoroughly.

In a day or two, when the glue is hard and see-through, carefully peel the shapes from the wax paper.

Decorate the shapes with fine-lined colored markers on either side (one side will feel smoother because it wasn't in contact with the waxed paper). Hang the colored pieces in the window as stained glass. They also make great Christmas tree ornaments and package decorations.

• Birdseed Pretzels •

(PLATES 7–8)

Skills rating: Easy
An easy cleanup project

Want a wonderful way to draw a wintertime crowd of feathered friends? Make birdseed pretzels.

On a flat piece of wax paper, squirt nontoxic white glue into fat lines that form pretzel-like shapes. Be sure the lines are wide enough (at least $\frac{1}{4}$ inch). Also be sure to make all the lines meet, just as real pretzels do.

Sprinkle birdseed or sunflower seeds onto the glue. Be generous. Later you can pour off the excess and use it again.

Allow it to dry for a day or two.

Then carefully peel away the pretzels from the waxed paper. Hang your bird bounty on tree branches (secure the pretzels by tying with thread, if desired).

Chapter II

Raised Glue Designs and Relief Prints

• Raised Glue Designs •

(PLATES 9–14)

Skills rating: Easy to moderate
An easy cleanup project

Bright, beautiful markers are always a favorite art medium. Now boring old white glue has been colorized too. There are a number of decorative colored glues on the market. One is Elmer's GluColors™, available in a variety of neon colors.

You can make your own custom-colored glue with ordinary food coloring. Add several drops directly to white glue in its bottle, and mix well. When you tire of using red glue, or yellow glue, or blue glue, then create an intermediate, or tertiary, color. After that, produce a secondary color in the very same glue bottle. For example, the addition of a little red coloring to yellow glue makes a lovely yellow-orange color. The addition of a bit more red dye produces orange.

To make a colorful glue design to be enhanced later with markers, you'll first need white tagboard or sturdy paper, 9 × 12 inches or larger. With glue bottle in hand, squeeze out a continuous line using some control—not just aimless squiggles. Try spirals, sunbursts, or other patterns. Leave some open spaces in a variety of sizes. That's not to say there can't be some puddles of glue filling in some spaces—that's okay. But do stay well within the borders of your background. Glue too near the edge may spread right off the page.

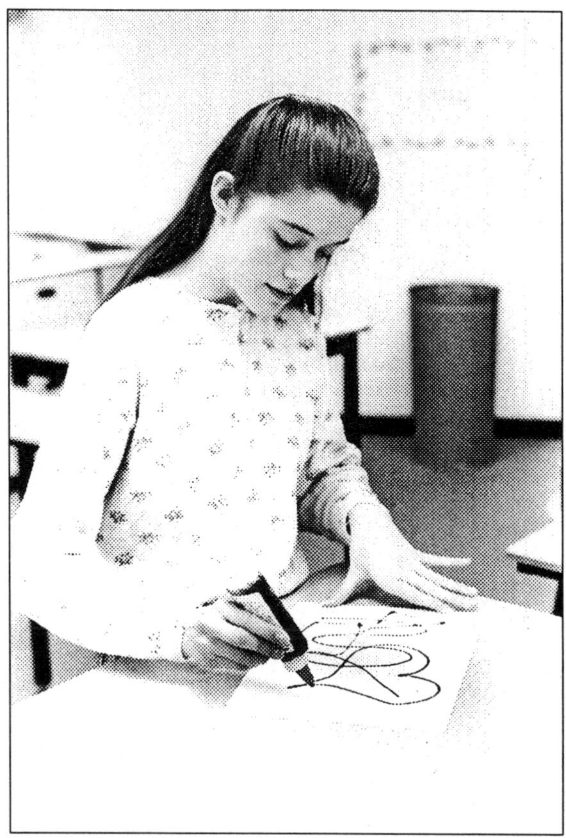

Student creating a black-(or colored) glue design

Set the work in progress aside to dry for an entire day or more. Then assemble your markers and felt-tipped pens: Fat ones, skinny ones, fine-point, wide-nibbed—gather a group of colorful ones. Choose colors that are either related to your glue colors or that accent them. Run marker lines along some of the edges of raised glue. Fill in some background shapes with either solid colors or with patterns. Use stripes, dots, zigzags, checkerboard squares—you name it.

Raised glue literally adds another dimension to these designs. Glue and markers make perfect partners.

Evaluation

Do the glue lines and shapes form a pleasing composition? Are some lines bold, others fine? Do the colors work well together? Have you used pattern to add interest?

• Relief Prints: Two Methods •

(PLATES 15–18)

Skills rating: Easy to moderate
An easy cleanup project

Method One

Use your glue-and-marker design from the first part of this chapter to take a rubbing. It won't harm your original, and you can make as many copies as you wish.

Place a piece of paper (white or light-colored) over your dried-glue design. A pad of thick newspapers underneath everything helps too. Peel some crayons (take the paper wrappers off). Hold your papers down with one hand and, with the other hand, use a crayon sideways (flat) to make a rubbing. Experiment by turning the page slightly and re-rubbing with a variety of colors.

Method Two

Another printmaking technique does ruin your original, so don't use this method unless you're willing to ink up your glue design.

You'll need water-base printing ink, a brayer (ink roller), papers to print on, and a flat surface to spread the ink upon.

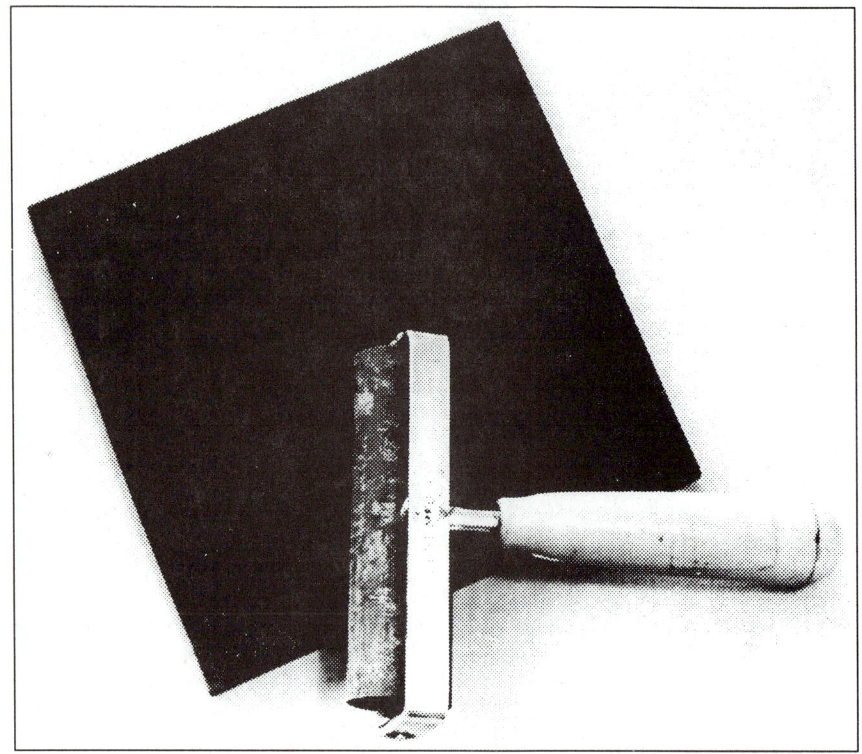

Ink brayer

Squeeze out a little ink and roll the brayer in it until evenly coated. Then ink up your raised-glue lines and shapes. It's nearly impossible to keep from getting a little ink on your background. In fact, such accidents are part of the process, so don't worry about them.

Quickly place your printing paper on top of the inked glue and press all over the back with the palm of your hand. Peel off and *voilá*! A raised-glue print. Try multiple prints (more than one on a single sheet of paper), and try different-colored inks and background combinations.

Evaluation

Does the print have clarity and contrast? Are the colors attractive together? Have you effectively explored the possibilities of multiple prints?

Chapter III

Glue and Pastels—A Dynamic Duo

(PLATES 19–24)

Skills rating: Easy to advanced
An easy cleanup project

For this mixed-media project, you'll need:

- Dispense bottle of clear glue or white glue
- Black construction paper 9 × 12 or 12 × 18 inches
- Colored chalk pastels
- Art gum eraser
- Fixative

First, produce a well-balanced composition in glue on a black background sheet. If working nonobjectively, use only lines and shapes. Patterns are fine to use too—dots, zigzags, and others. Try to avoid huge "lakes" of glue, though. Remember, glue spreads, so avoid the edges of your paper with your glue design.

In a day or two, come back to your dried artwork. Clear glue like LePage's® will have worked great for this, because the black paper underneath appears even blacker. If you used white glue, it's common for some of it to still appear milky rather than transparent.

Get out your colored chalk pastels and choose a color scheme. It might be all warms (reds, yellows, oranges, warm browns), or it might be the cool colors (blues, greens, and violets). The possibilities are many. Whatever the

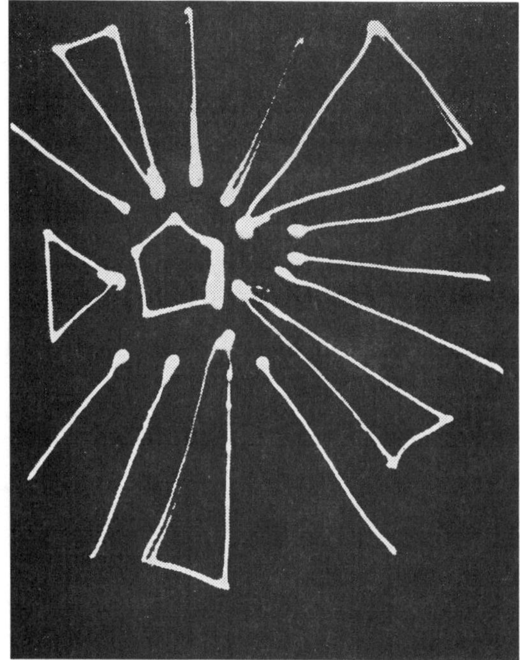
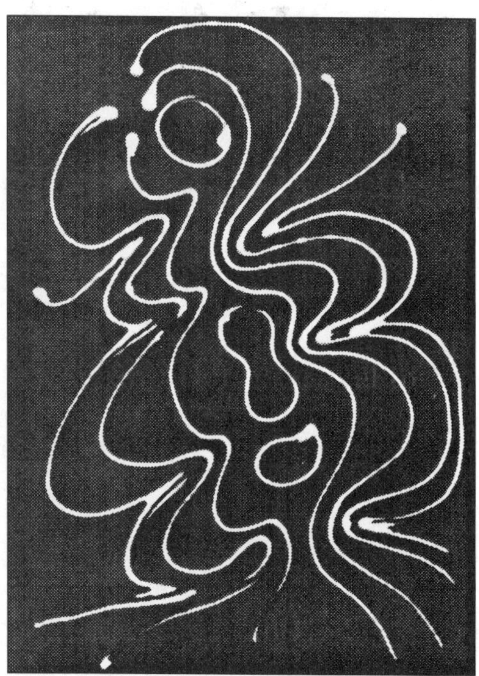

White glue on black paper, before chalk pastels are added

scheme, be sure to add black and white to your color choices, for a full range of values.

Now start chalking. You can work inside or outside the boundaries of the raised glue outlines. You can even fill the entire page with chalk, rubbing the surface to create a resist effect. Remember that pastels are made for blending and mixing. Create some highlighted areas as focal points in your design, and try to maintain a center of interest.

Finally, erase stray fingerprints and spray the completed artwork with fixative to prevent smearing. Hair spray can substitute for the commercial fixative. (A light spray is sufficient, not a drenching.)

A black background accents bright chalk beautifully, but it is not the only option. Try colored construction paper or white paper or tagboard. In the case of the latter, experiment with colored glue (see Chapter II). Whatever the background, glue and pastels make a pretty pair.

Evaluation

Does the glue design exhibit an interesting variety of sizes, shapes, and lines? Does it have unity? Have you used an ideal combination of colors and values? Have you achieved good contrast between lights and darks?

Chapter IV

Black Glue: A Winner with Watercolors

(PLATES 25–33)

Skills rating: Easy to advanced

Black, viscous lines oozing onto white paper or tagboard—what fun! You can make black glue by adding one third india ink to two thirds white liquid glue. Mix well. Commercially, black glue is available from the Conros Corporation: Ross® Colored Playtime Glue.

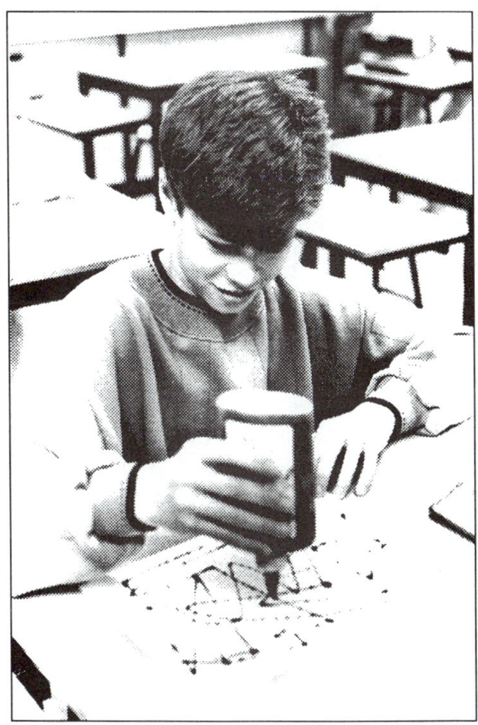

Student creating a colored-glue (or black-glue) design

Note: Don't use washable school glue—it becomes rubbery and difficult to work with when india ink is added to it.

Use the sticky black mixture as the basis for a nonobjective design or a representational picture. On a white background (9 × 12 inches or larger) squeeze out a line drawing in black glue. If you feel the need, you may draw light lines in pencil first. (It is also possible to do this activity with white glue on white paper, or even with colored glue.)

Freehand or over pencil lines, move the glue bottle fairly quickly as you create a design on paper. The glue line may widen, drip, or puddle in places. Leave those unintended effects as they are. They can add charm to an artwork. But do stay well within the borders of your support. If you avoid the edges, you'll help prevent the glue from spreading off the sides..

As you continue, outline some shapes and fill in others with solid glue. You may choose angular lines and shapes that are square, rectangular, or

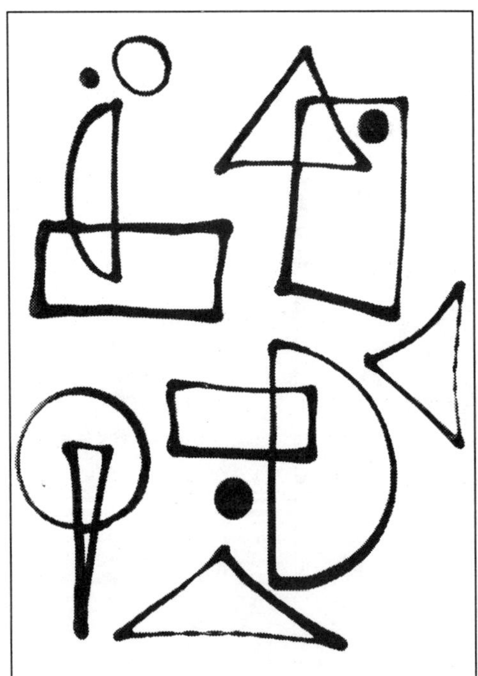

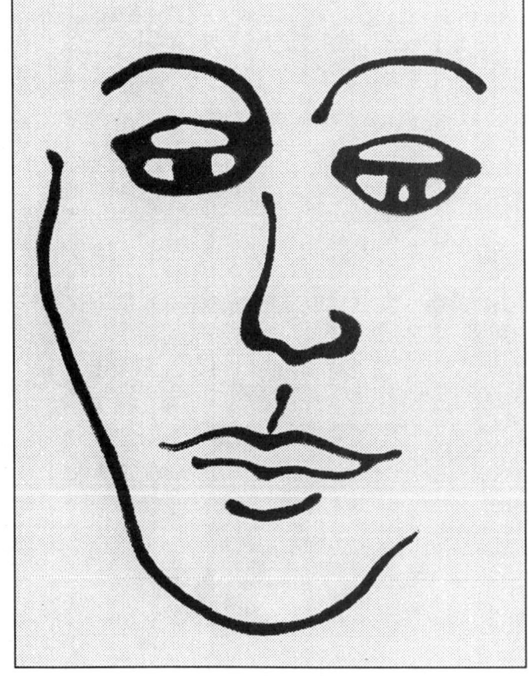

Black-glue designs before watercolors are added

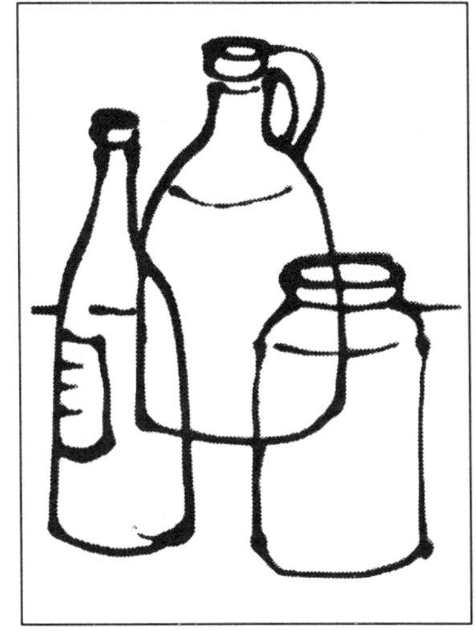

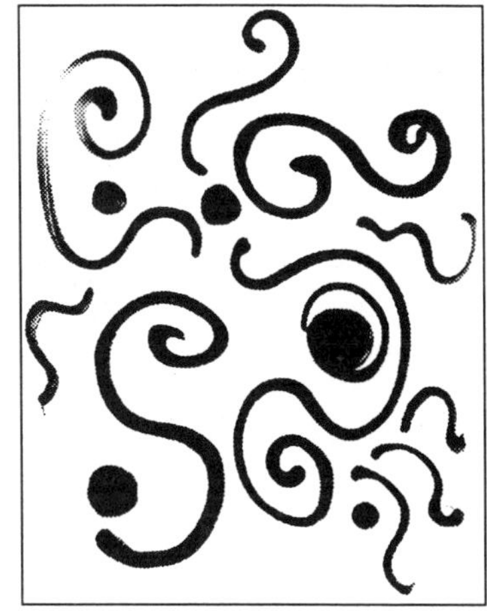

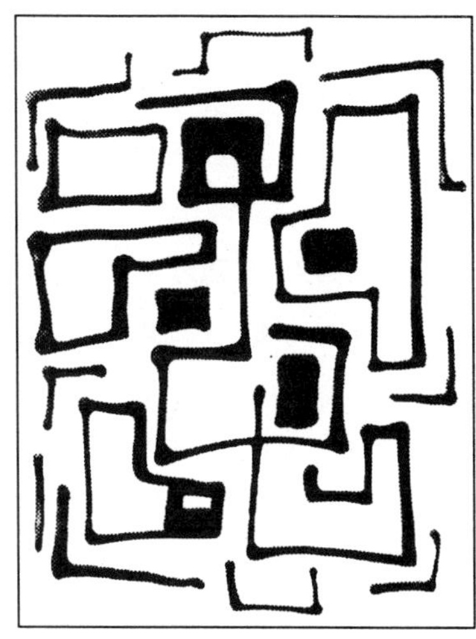

Black-glue designs before watercolors are added

triangular. You may use flowing, rounded lines and shapes. Or you may use a combination of both types. You may feel most comfortable with recognizable shapes like a flower, an interesting insect, a fancy fish, or a bird. Don't try to clean up any accidental drips or goofs.

Set the glue design aside to dry until it is hard, which should be in a day or two. Then "get set"—get out your watercolor paint set, that is.

You'll notice that the black lines have a slightly raised surface that adds a nice tactile quality. The colors you'll use next will seem brighter and more intense next to the black accent lines. And the raised lines will help to keep different areas of watercolor from running into each other.

Choose a well-planned color scheme with a limited number of paint colors. Families of related colors look pretty together. Paint them around, in, and over the black glue. Colored inks, tempera, or acrylic paints make fine substitutes for watercolors. Try some experimenting with "black-glue beauties" and you'll see: Black glue is great.

Black outlines have been used in the past by artists such as Georges Rouault, Paul Klee, Joan Miró, and Jackson Pollock.

Evaluation

Does the design present a fluidity and a freedom of expression? Does the watercolor painting demonstrate transparency? Do you see the dramatic impact of black contrasted with brilliant color?

Chapter V

Rubber Cement Resist—Remarkable!

(Plates 34–40)

Skills rating: Moderate to advanced

It's sensational stuff—slippery and slimy! Use rubber cement as the basis for a great mixed-media painting. You'll need white drawing paper (9 × 12 inches or larger), a watercolor paint set, water container, and black markers or black india ink. And, of course, rubber cement.

Note: Rubber cement could irritate eyes and skin. Be careful not to inhale the vapors. Use good ventilation.

First, use the applicator brush with the rubber cement to stroke a design onto the white paper. Make swirly organic shapes and lines, geometric ones, or even a representational picture. Flowers, butterflies, fish—let your imagination flow as freely as the cement.

Next, use your paint brush to wash brilliant watercolor over your paper. You don't even have to wait for the cement to dry. Choose a pleasing color scheme, and fill your brush with lots of wet paint. Lightly paint with smooth strokes over the rubber cement and all. Droplets of watercolor will bead up on the cemented areas like water on a duck's feathers. When finished with this part of the design-making, set aside to dry.

Soon you'll be able to complete the next step. Rub at the cement lines and shapes with your thumb and fingers. Put some elbow grease into it and rub the cement right off the page. Keep up the friction until the paper feels smooth, not sticky.

Removing the resist material with your hands leaves white, unpainted areas. Don't be alarmed if you see some colored specks in the white areas. A few spots of watercolor paint here and there are okay. They're a part of the process and add a nice texture.

The final touch is to accent the painting with black lines. Use markers or felt-tipped pens in several sizes. You may wish to substitute black india ink, applied with a fine brush. Outline some of the shapes with both thick and thin lines. Defining some edges like this, tying together some of the shapes, adds interest and unity.

When you're done, display your masterpiece on a black background to bring out the accent lines.

Evaluation

Have you used a variety of lines—long and short, fat and skinny, straight and bent—in different directions? Is the arrangement satisfying and the color scheme harmonious? Have you displayed a knowledge of watercolor washes?

Chapter VI

Glue Collage and Turpentine Resist

(Plates 41–46)

Skills rating: Advanced
Artful recycling

Glue can resist the action of color-removing turpentine, just as rubber cement resisted the watercolor in Chapter V. Here's how to make a magazine paper collage with the resist technique added for more interest.

For a sturdy support, use cardboard or posterboard ($8\frac{1}{2} \times 11$ inches). Choose a theme or motif for your collage—something of interest to you, like sports, music, or even foods. More seriously, you might portray a social message, speaking out for ecology or another such cause.

When you've chosen your subject matter, find appropriate magazine pictures and words, in colors that seem to match your motif. For example, use team colors if you're making a sports collage. Tear out the magazine pictures, or cut them out with scissors. If you cut them, shapes may be either rounded and free-form or geometric.

Gather enough pictures, words, or even simply colored shapes to fill your cardboard background completely. First, arrange your pieces in an interesting, balanced way, and use overlapping. Then glue them down. Pay special attention to the edges: Glue them down thoroughly.

Next, squeeze out lines and shapes of white or clear glue onto the collage. You can outline some existing shapes (tracing the contours of a human figure, for instance). You can fill in parts of other photos with glue

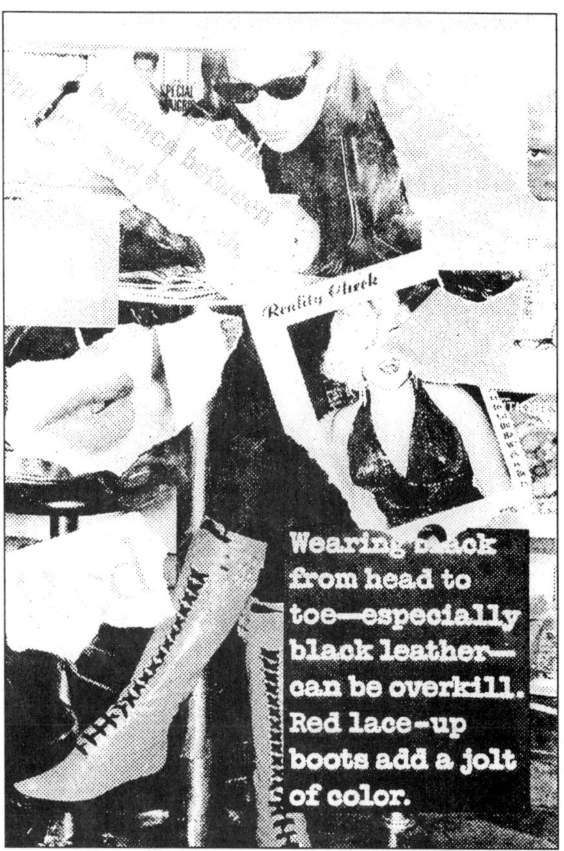

Magazine-picture collage before glue is added

(covering a model's face completely with a glue puddle, for example). Place interesting squiggles and glue shapes wherever there are words and colors you wish to save.

Remember that every portion of the collage that is covered with glue will be preserved; it will show later when the glue dries clear. The opposite is true of anything you do not cover with glue. Again, anything not protected with glue will be lost later, so do enough with your squeeze bottle now.

Set your sticky collage aside to dry, and come back to it the next day. You'll need a piece of cloth well-dampened with turpentine or lacquer thinner.

Note: These are very harmful if swallowed. Avoid contact with skin or eyes. Keep the area well ventilated.

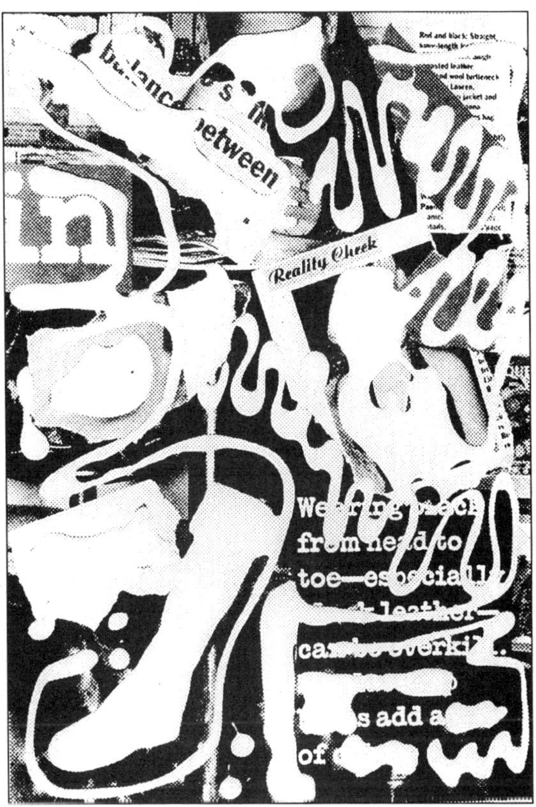

Magazine-picture collage immediately after glue is added

Work on top of some old newspapers, and use the rag with the solvent to scrub at your collage. This will remove the color from the unprotected parts of the magazine papers. Keep rubbing until you've faded the background considerably. (Use the same elbow grease you needed to remove the rubber cement in Chapter V.)

The color of some very high-quality, glossy magazine papers does not lift off no matter how hard you scrub. And, if you're not careful, you may find some magazine pieces peeling up at the edges and even some glue pieces popping off. Finally, don't be surprised if parts of your papers become see-through—turpentine sometimes makes papers semitransparent. It only adds interest.

Try an ir-resist-ible collage soon.

Evaluation

Assessment is based partly on emotional content. Have you a message to impart to the viewer? Are the colors appropriate to your topic? Is the finished work barren in places, or have you generated enough interest? Is there a center of interest?

Chapter VII

Tip-Top Tissue and Crepe Paper Too

• Tissue's the Tops •

(Plates 47–51)

Skills rating: All levels

A simpler collage, much faster and easier than the one in the previous chapter, uses a glue-and-water mixture with colored tissue paper. Just as the rubber cement-resist project in Chapter V could be representational or abstract, so too can this artwork. You can cut or tear tissue paper into geometric or free-form shapes, or you can assemble such recognizable shapes as hearts and arrows, a bouquet in a vase, or whatever you wish.

Use sturdy paper, tagboard, cardboard, or mat board as a support. A light-colored background would be best for colorful results. Mix white liquid glue with a little water to thin it (you may substitute polymer medium or decoupage glue if you have it). You'll also need a brush and some newspapers to spread underneath your work.

Choose four or five colors of tissue paper that will work well together. A well-planned color scheme is especially important when colors overlap and show through each other, as they will with this activity.

Next, cut or tear a variety of related shapes in different sizes. Arrange them, overlapping, on your background piece until a pleasing design has been formed. Adhere the tissue pieces by first lifting them and brushing thinned glue (or medium) underneath them on the support itself. Then lay the pieces down and brush more mixture on top.

Thin tissue wrinkles easily, which is perfectly acceptable. Also, the dye in some brands of tissue will bleed or spread when wet, and that too is often very appealing.

If your finished composition is a blend of beautiful pastel colors, you may wish to stop right there. However, if your collage has been done in vibrant, deep or bright colors, you may wish to accent it with a few touches of black india ink. Use a fine brush and a very light hand, and just follow along some edges of the paper shapes with a thin black line. The ink will branch out and spread a bit, so be careful not to overdo it. You'll be pleased with your totally terrific tissue collage. It's a top-notch idea.

Evaluation

Have your overlapped many transparent layers of tissue effectively? Have you used small, medium, and large pieces? Do the colors combine well? Are there focal points within the composition? Are there a variety of values in evidence?

• Crepe Paper Appliqué •

(Plates 52–54)

Skills rating: All levels

Sometimes artistic expression can come from almost accidental effects. Crepe paper prints are surprising and fun.

You'll need:

- Crepe paper in bright and/or deep colors
- Paintbrushes

- Glue and water (or liquid starch)
- White drawing paper or tagboard
- Permanent markers or india ink
- Pencils

First, draw a sketch on the white paper in pencil. Suggested subjects might be a person, still-life objects, a large colorful insect, or a tropical fish. Go over the pencil lines in permanent ink (your choice of either marker or bushed-on india ink). Allow it to dry.

Next, wet the surface with a glue-and-water mixture (or with liquid laundry starch). Place torn or cut pieces of crepe paper on the white paper. The color should bleed, or run, especially if you brush more liquid over the top of the crepe paper pieces.

Sometimes the transfer of color is not satisfactory, either because the crepe paper color is very light or it is colorfast. Be sure to remove the moist crepe paper pieces while they still peel off easily. You may be delighted to see a wonderfully wrinkled print underneath.

Speaking of wrinkled, your background paper will buckle and curl up as it dries. Use heavier tagboard or even good watercolor paper, if available, for easier flattening of the work later.

Evaluation

Is the ink drawing well balanced on the page? Have you used good craftsmanship in drawing with the marker or with the brush and india ink? Have you chosen a pleasant color scheme? Are the color transfers effectively printed on the paper?

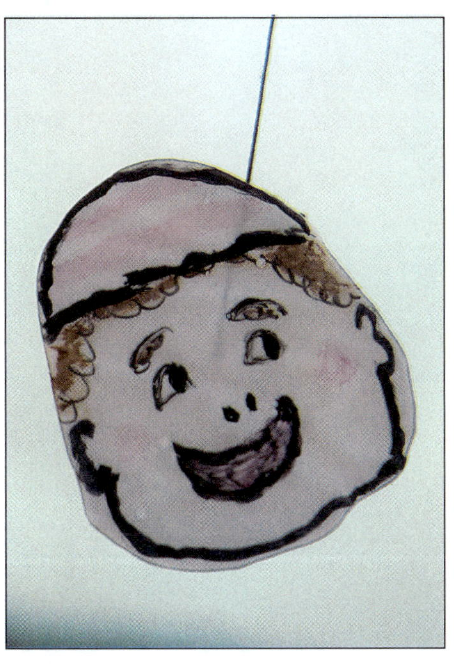

Plate 1. Light catcher or "sticky"

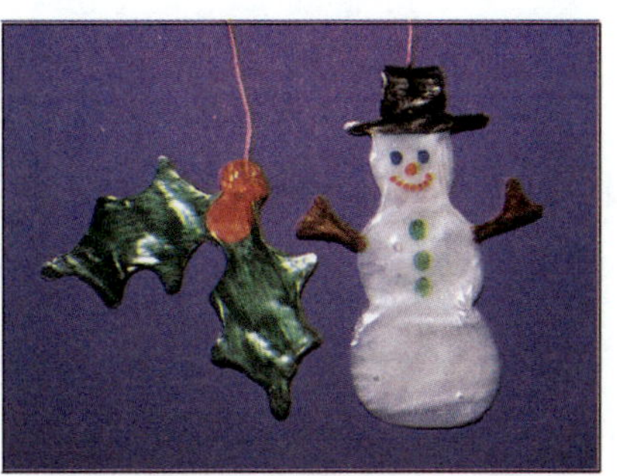

Plate 2. Light catcher or "sticky" snowman and holly

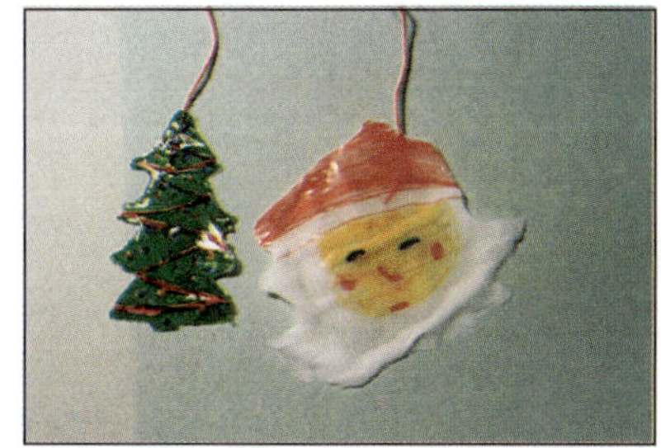

Plate 3. Light catcher or "sticky" Santa and Christmas tree

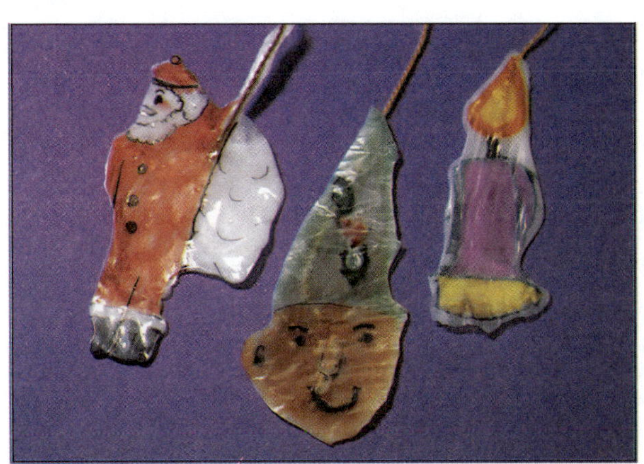

Plate 4. Light catcher or "sticky" holiday themes

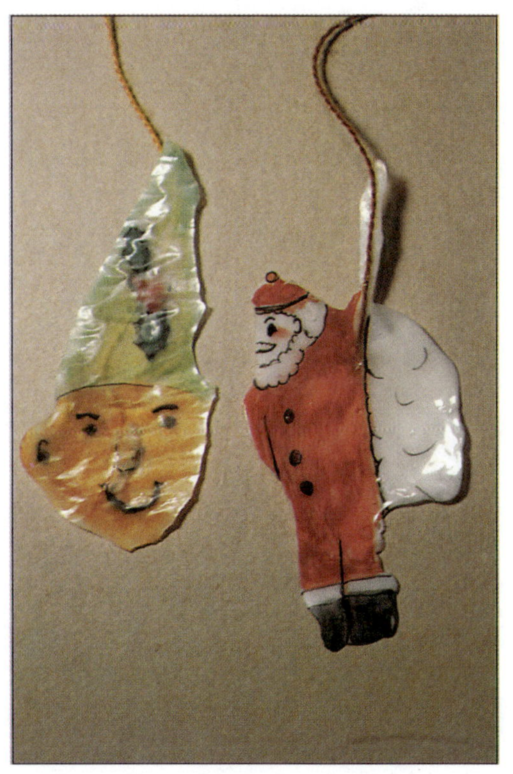

Plate 5. Light catcher or "sticky" holiday themes

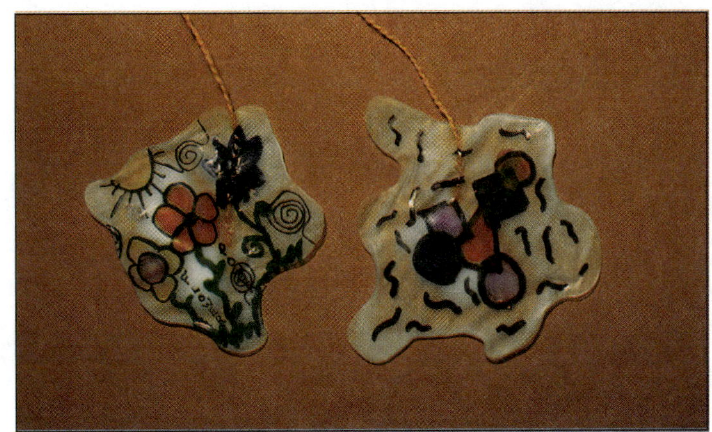

Plate 6. Light catcher or "sticky"

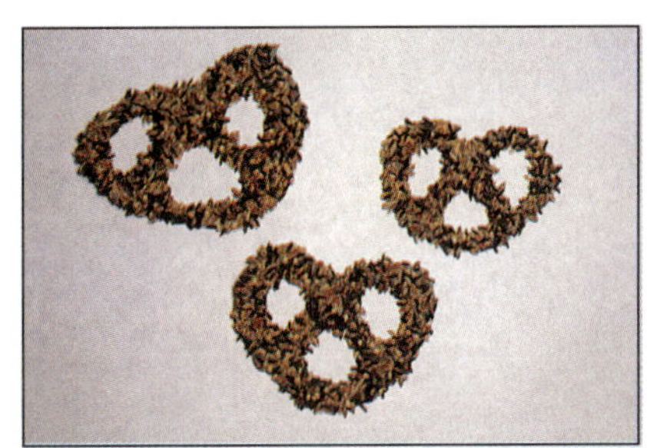

Plate 7. Bird pretzels

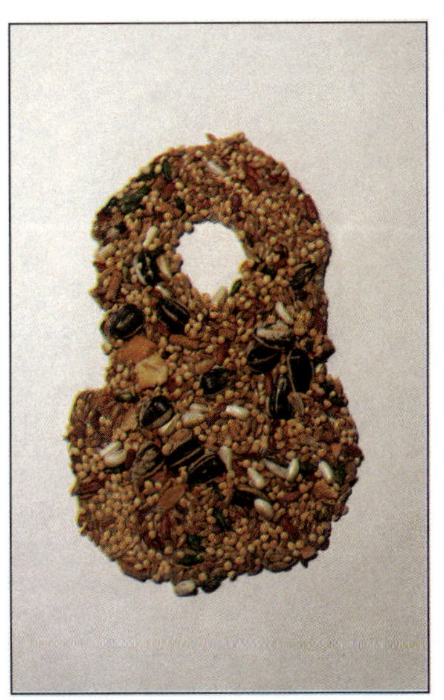

Plate 8. Large bird pretzel

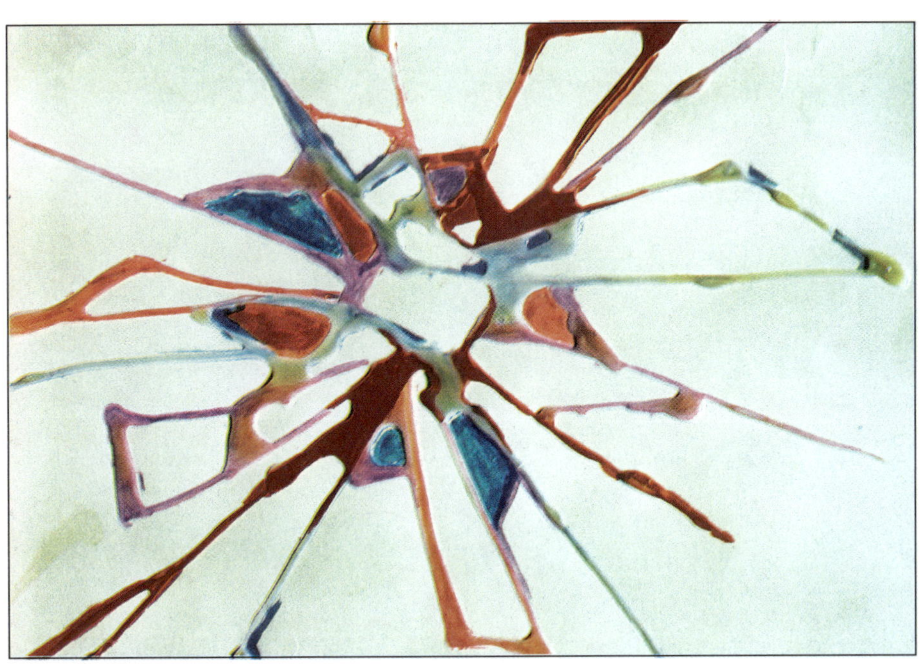

Plate 9. Colored glue design

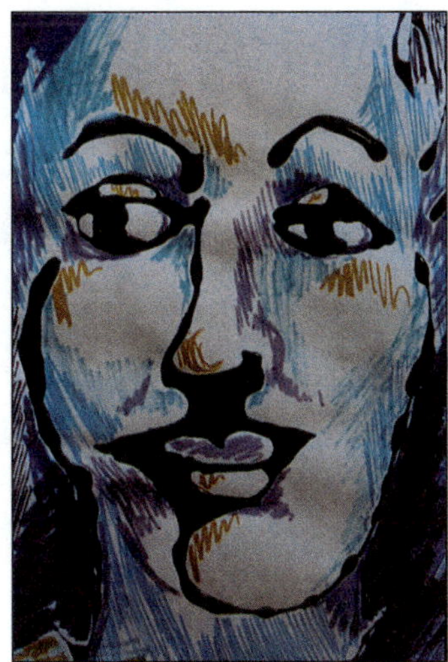

Plate 10. Colored glue with markers

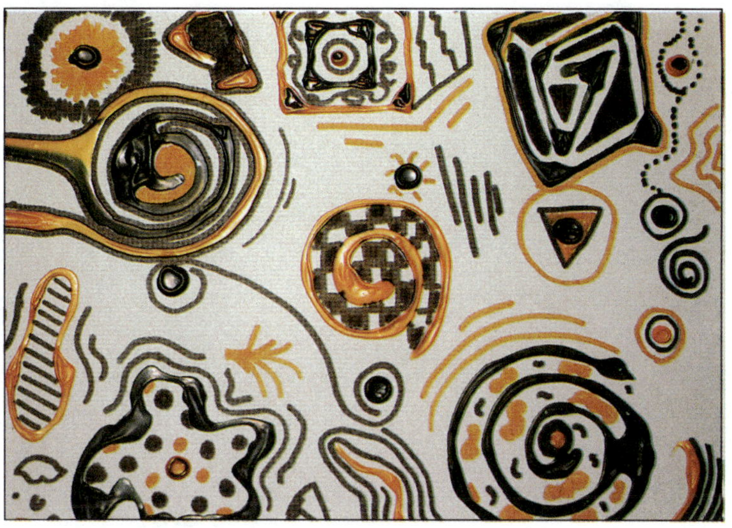

Plate 11. Colored glue with markers

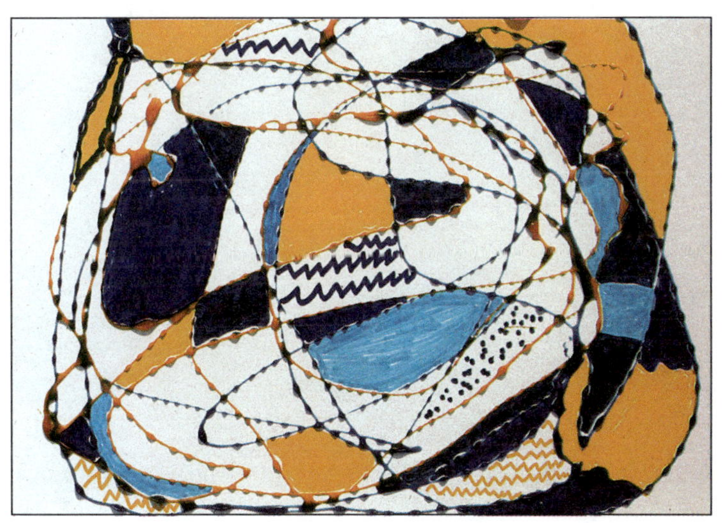

Plate 12. Colored glue with markers

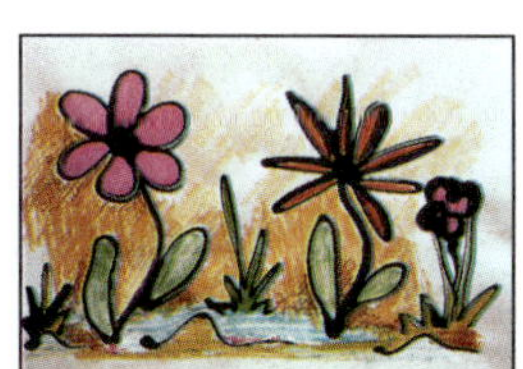

Plate 13. Colored glue with markers

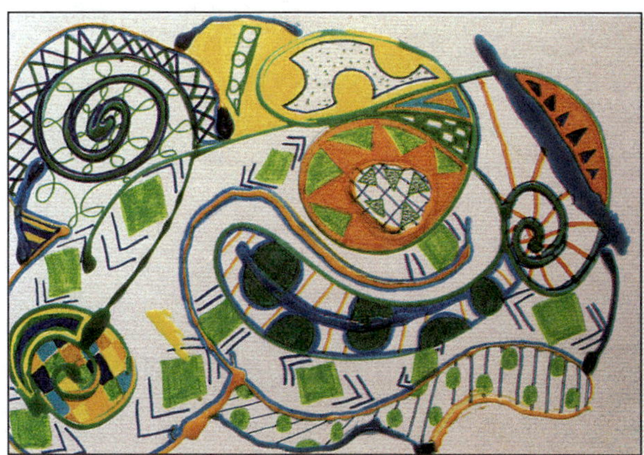

Plate 14. Colored glue with markers

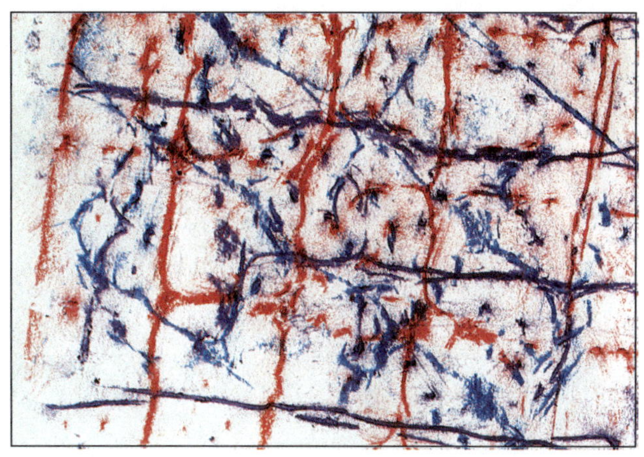

Plate 15. Rubbings from colored glue designs

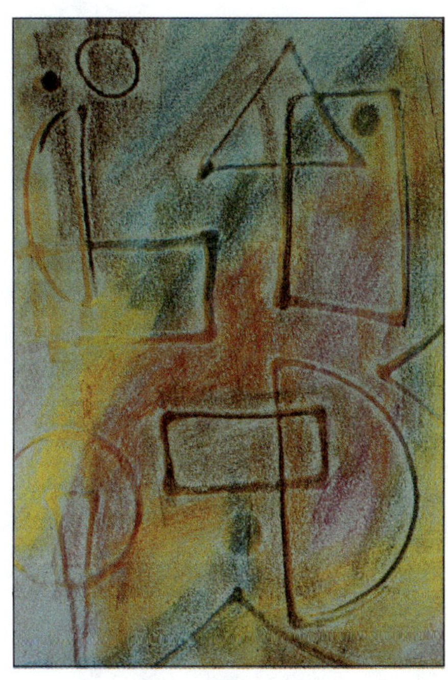

Plate 16. Rubbings from colored glue designs

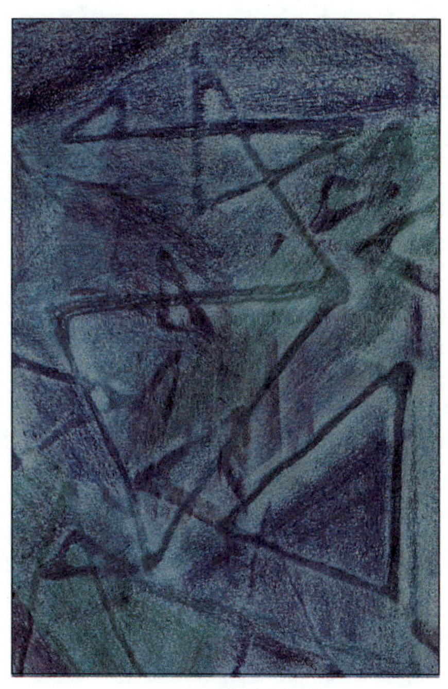

Plate 17. Rubbings from colored glue designs

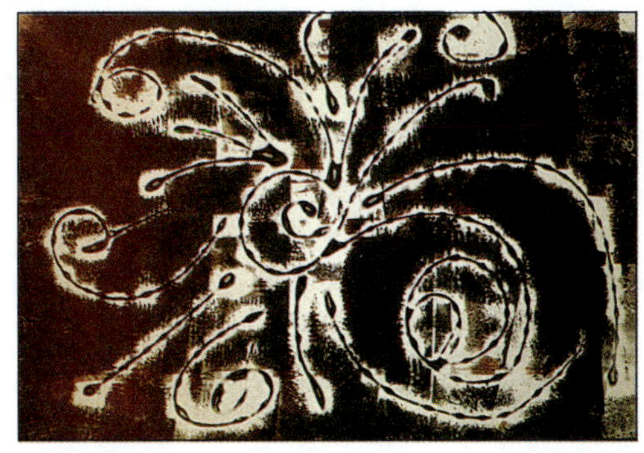

Plate 18. Inked print from raised glue design

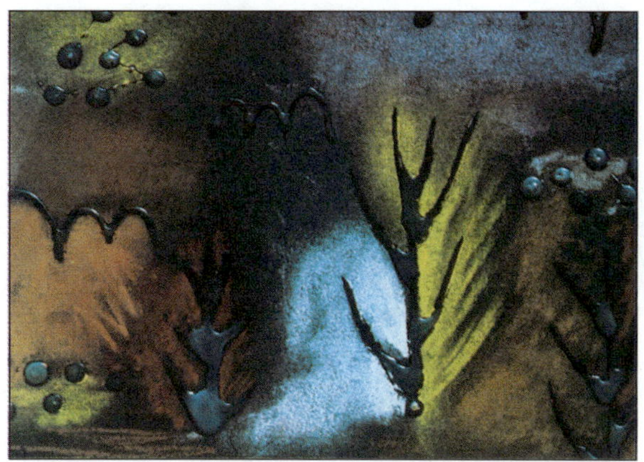

Plate 19. Glue and pastels on black paper

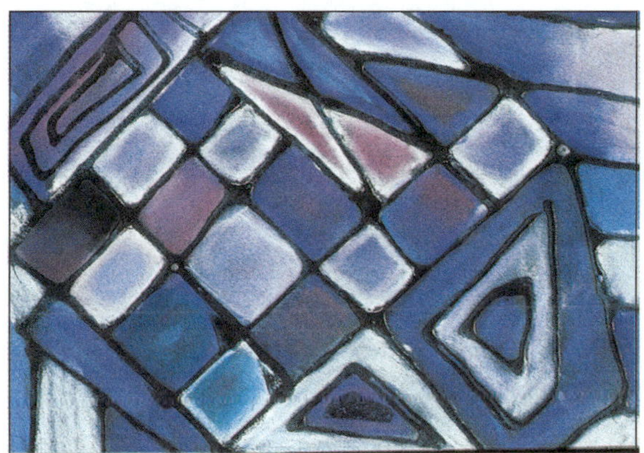

Plate 20. Glue and pastels on black paper

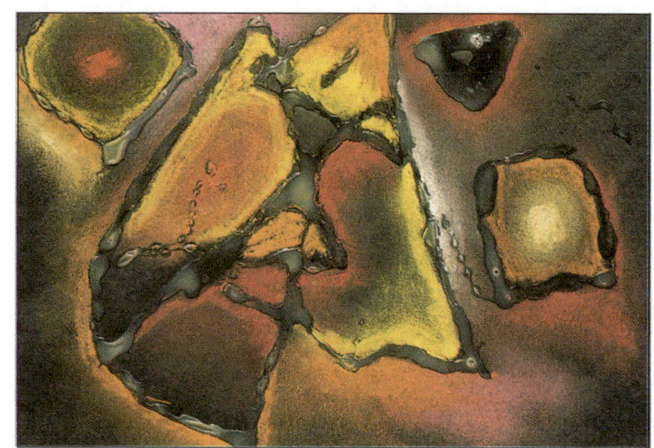

Plate 21. Glue and pastels on black paper

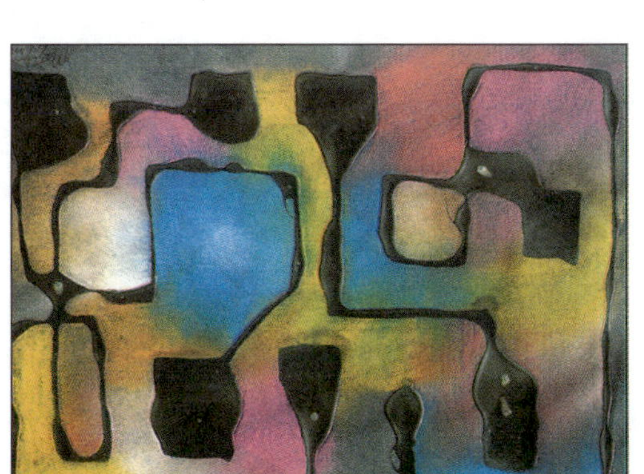

Plate 22. Glue and pastels on black paper

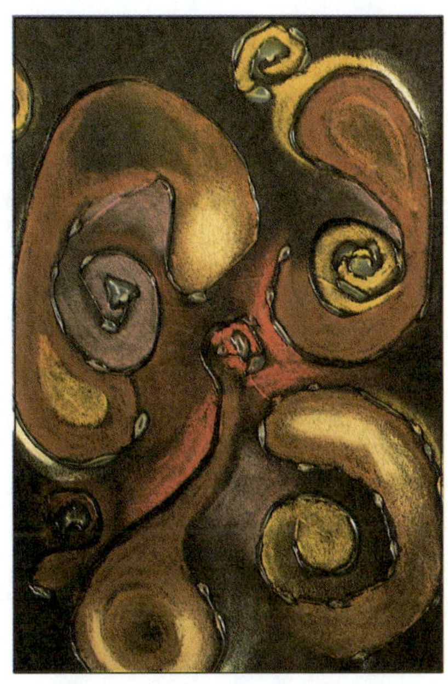

Plate 23. Glue and pastels on black paper

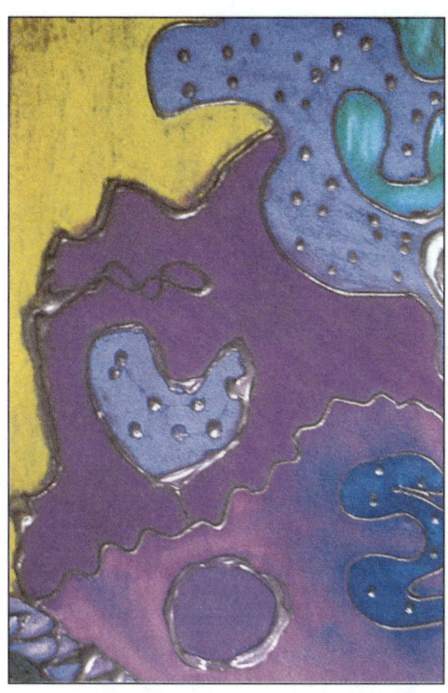

Plate 24. Glue and pastels on black paper

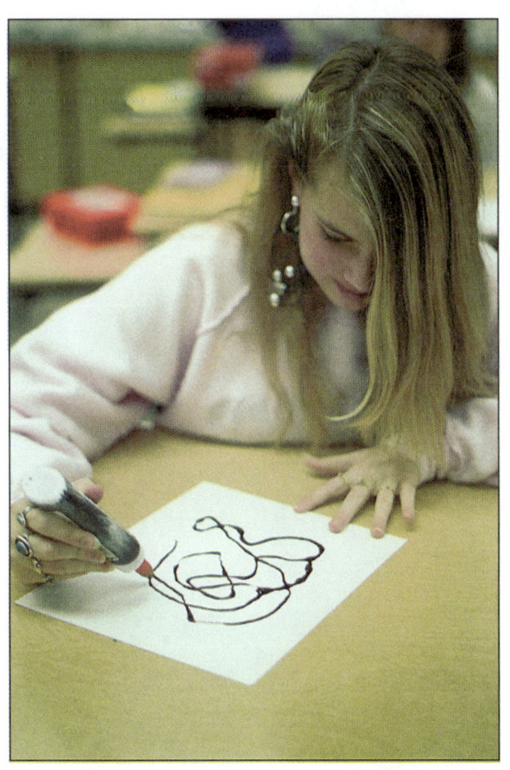

Plate 25. Student creating a black-glue design

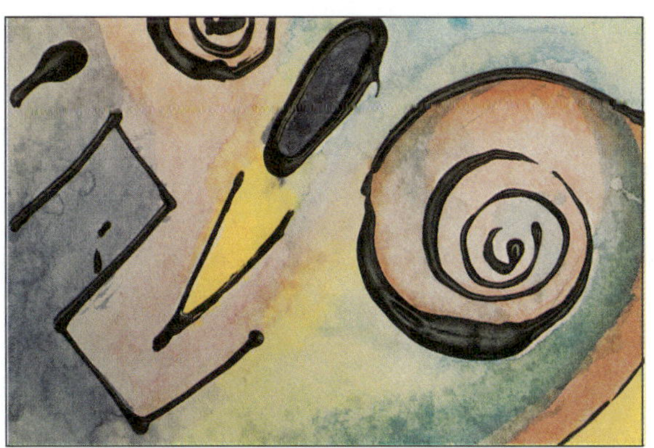

Plate 26. Black glue and watercolor

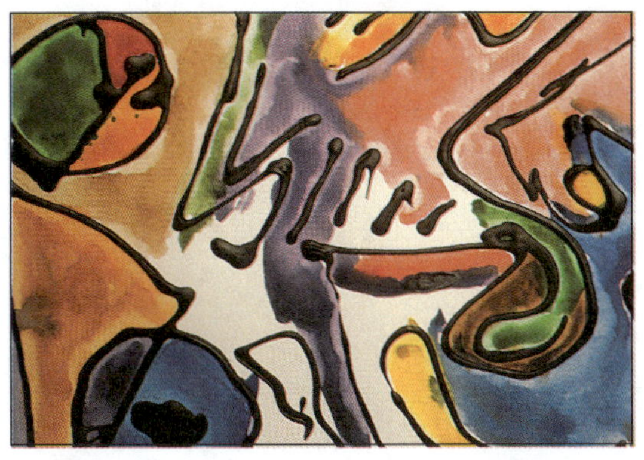

Plate 27. Black glue and watercolor

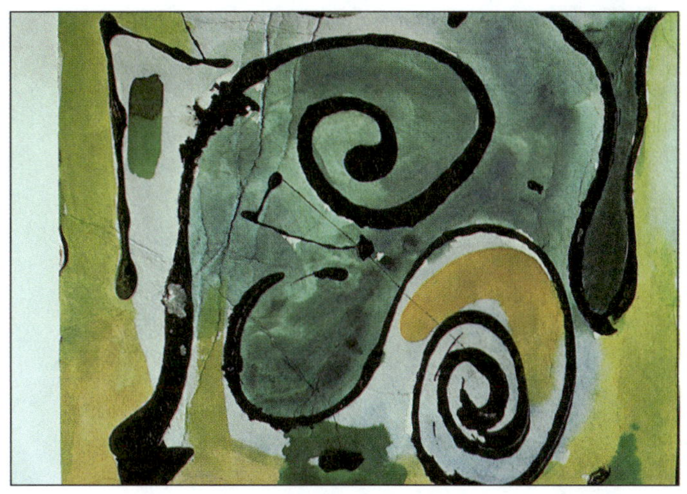

Plate 28. Black glue and watercolor

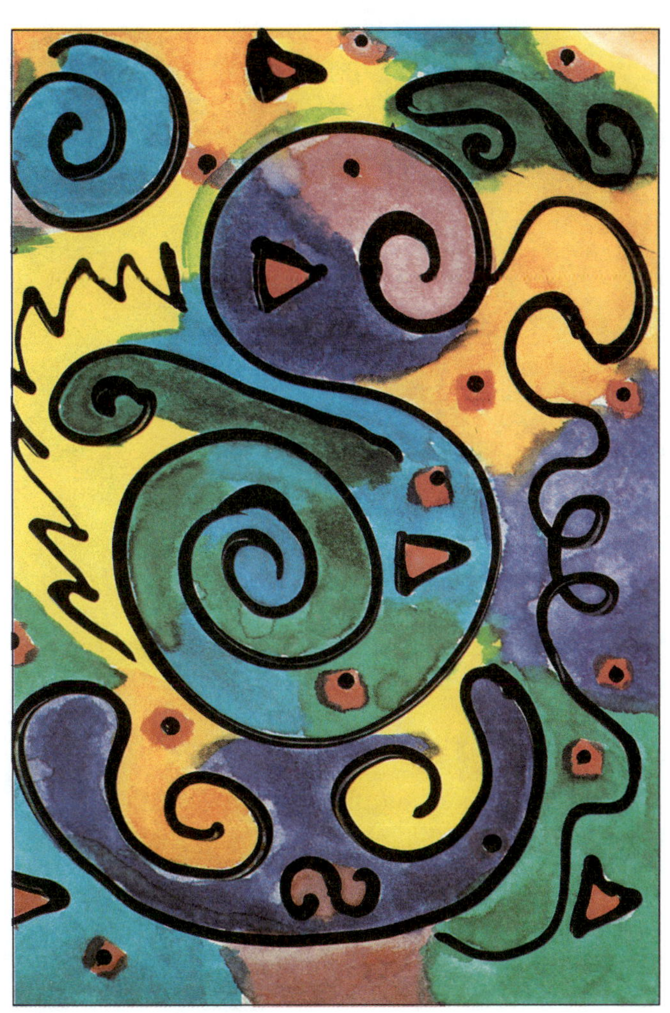

Plate 29. Black glue and watercolor

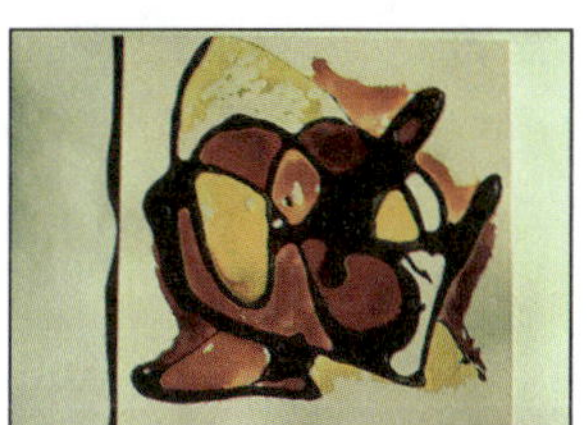

Plate 30. Black glue and watercolor

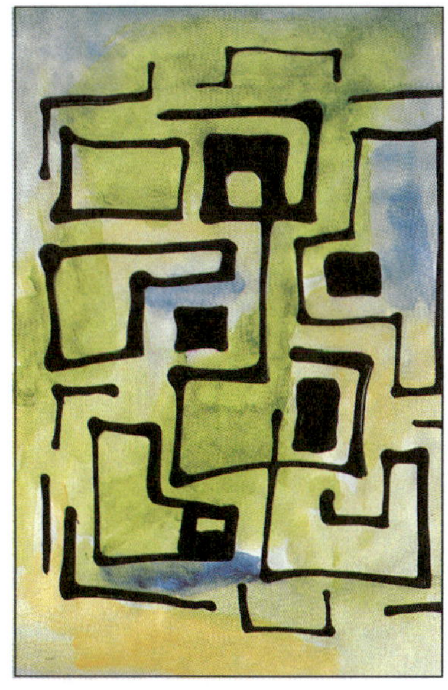

Plate 31. Black glue and watercolor

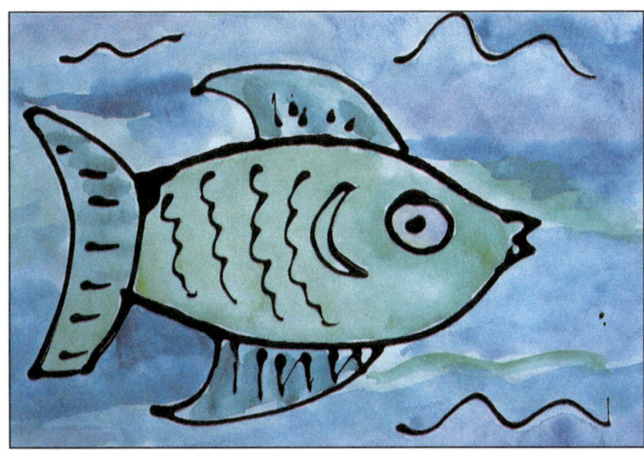

Plate 32. Black glue and watercolor

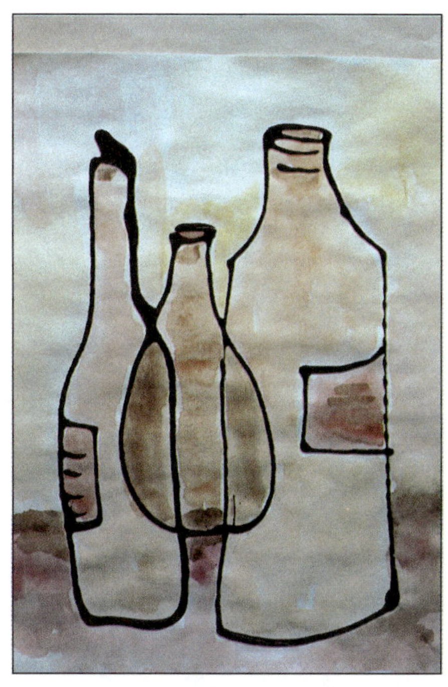

Plate 33. Black glue and watercolor

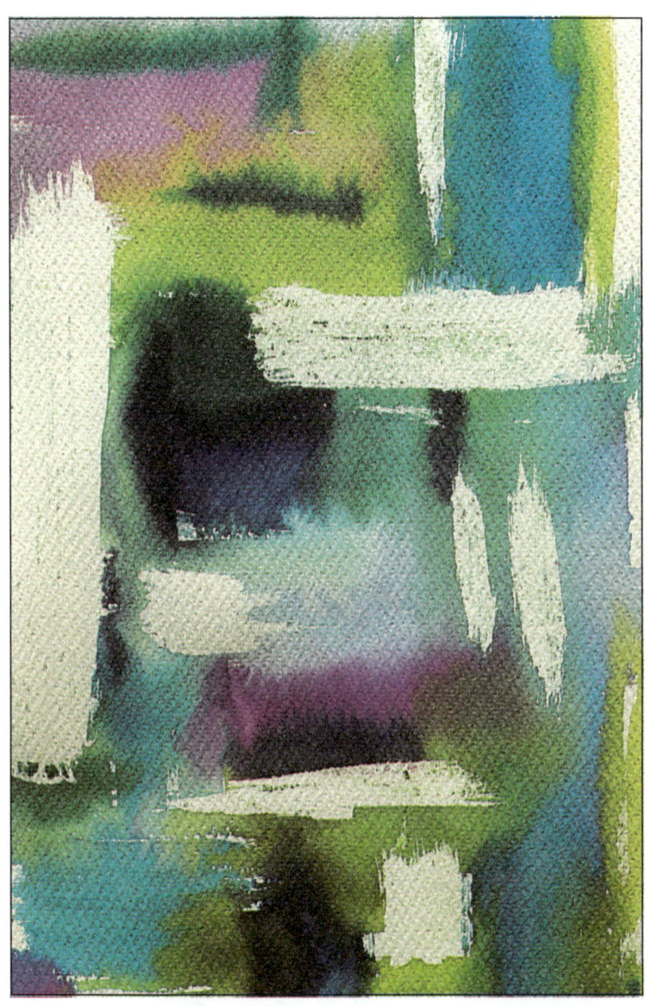

Plate 34. Rubber cement-resist with watercolor, *no* accent lines added in black yet

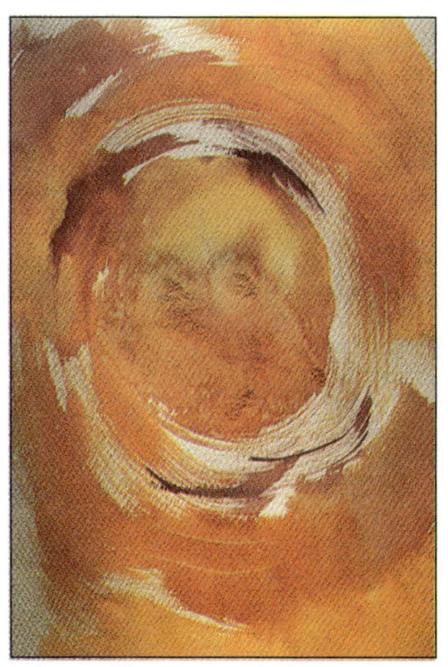

Plate 35. Rubber cement-resist with watercolor, *no* accent lines added in black yet

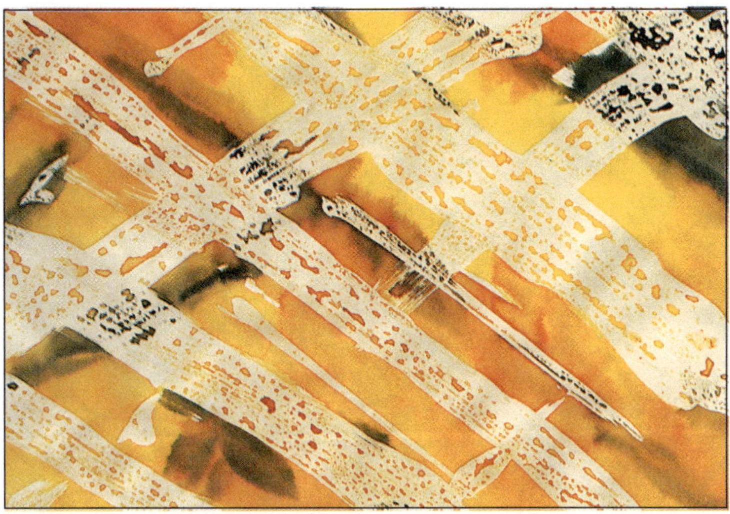

Plate 36. Rubber cement-resist with watercolor, *no* accent lines added in black yet

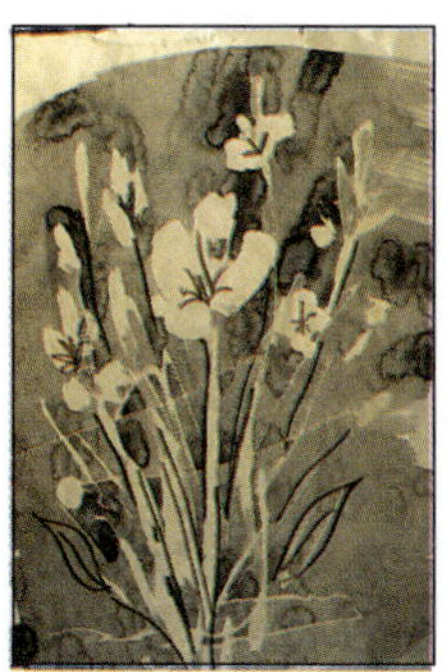

Plate 37. Rubber cement-resist, watercolor, **and black** accent lines

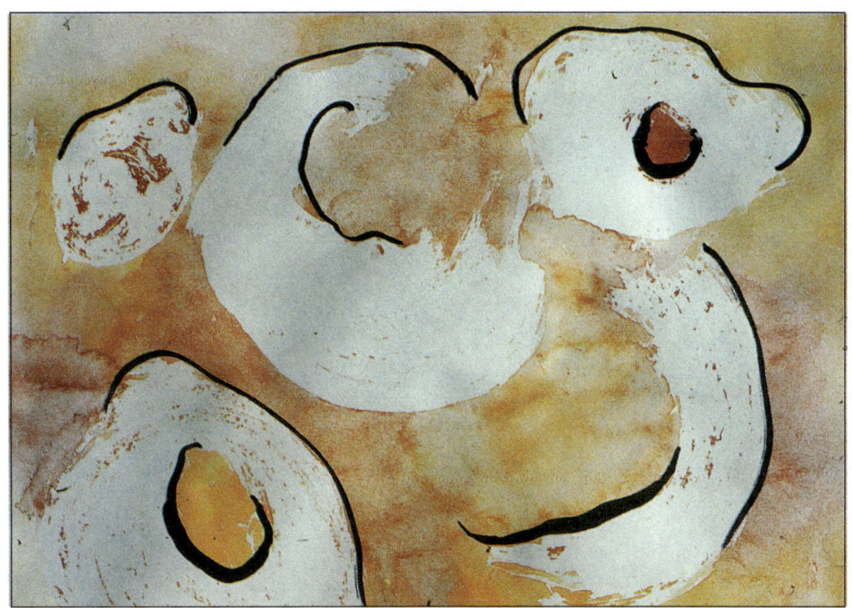

Plate 38. Rubber cement-resist, watercolor, and black accent lines

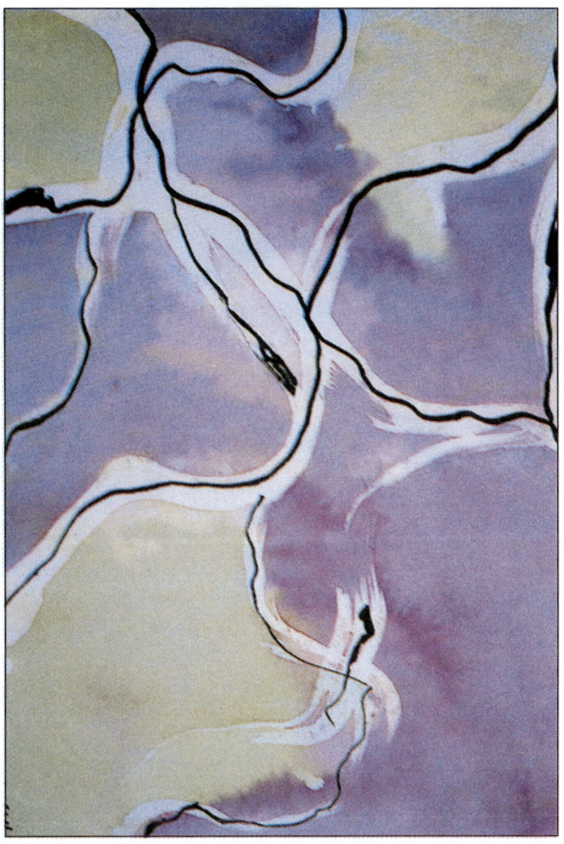

Plate 39. Rubber cement-resist, watercolor, and black accent lines

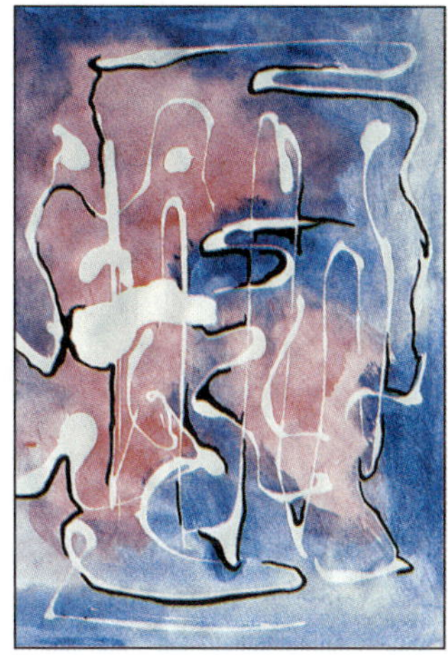

Plate 40. Rubber cement-resist, watercolor, and black accent lines

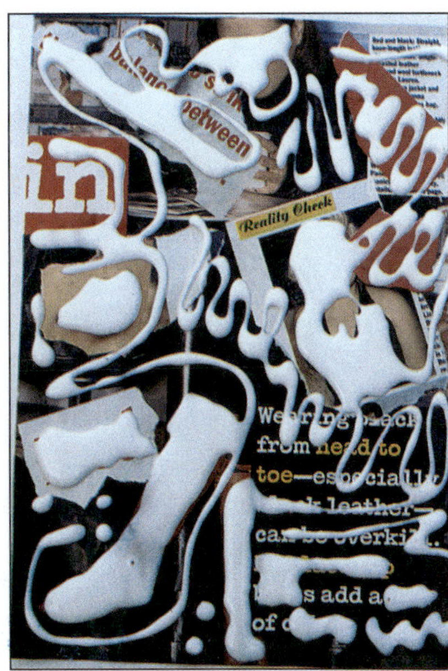

Plate 41. Magazine paper collage with glue recently added as resist (see photo of same)

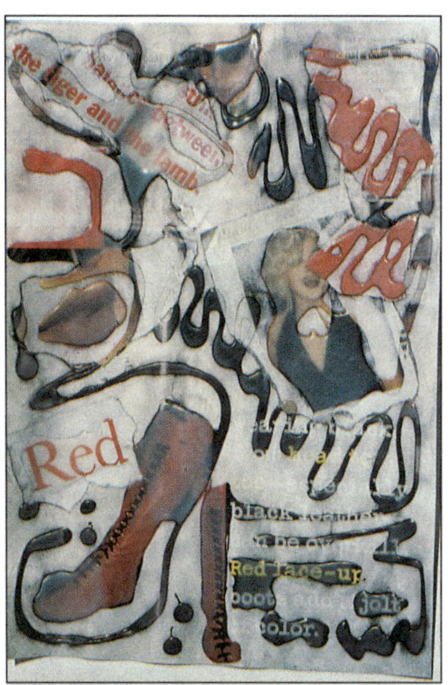

Plate 42. Same magazine collage as Plate 41, final stage (after removal of background color with turpentine)

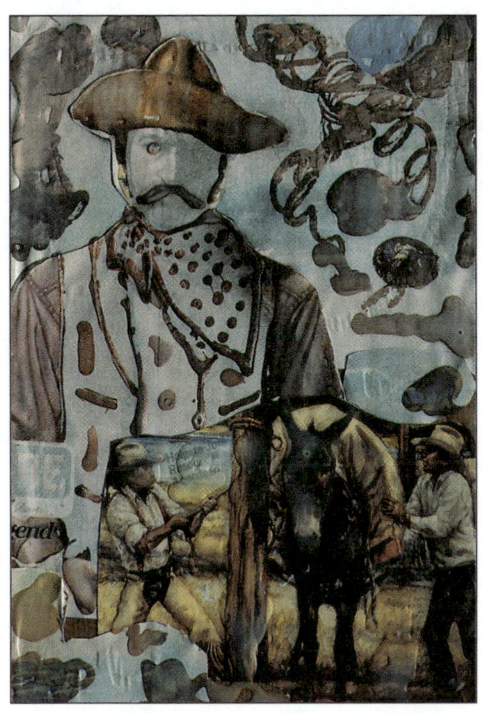

Plate 43. Glue collage with turpentine

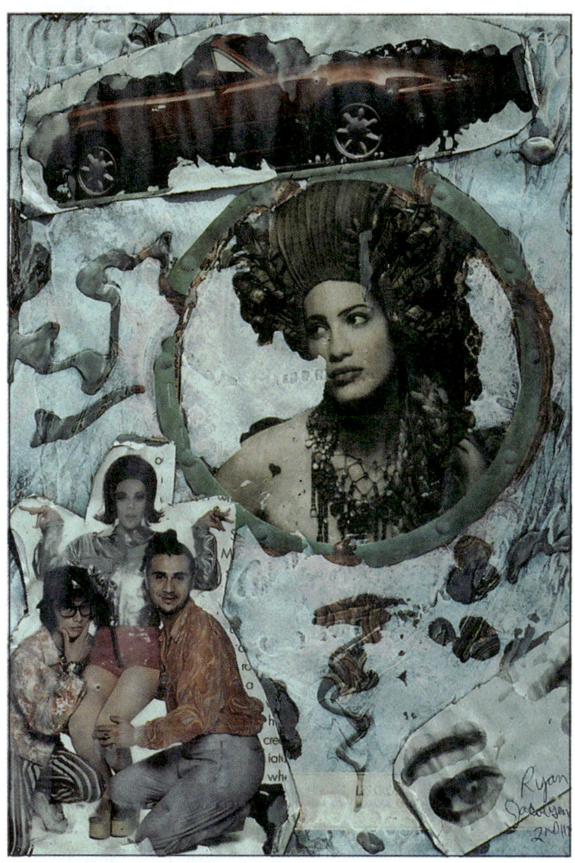

Plate 44. Glue collage with turpentine

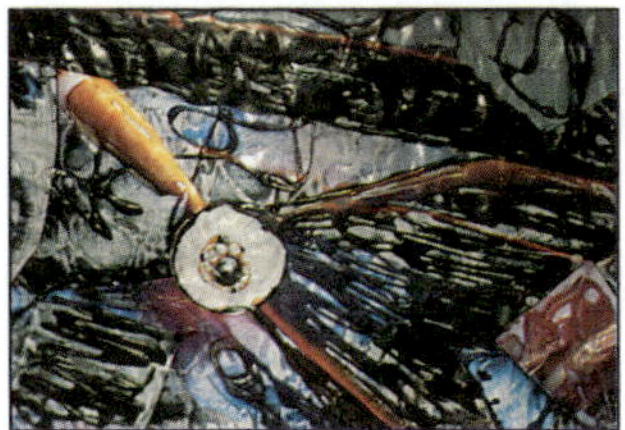

Plate 45. Glue collage with turpentine

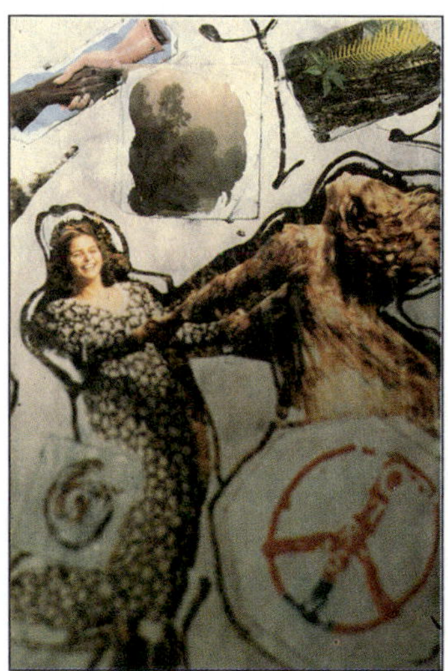

Plate 46. Glue collage with turpentine

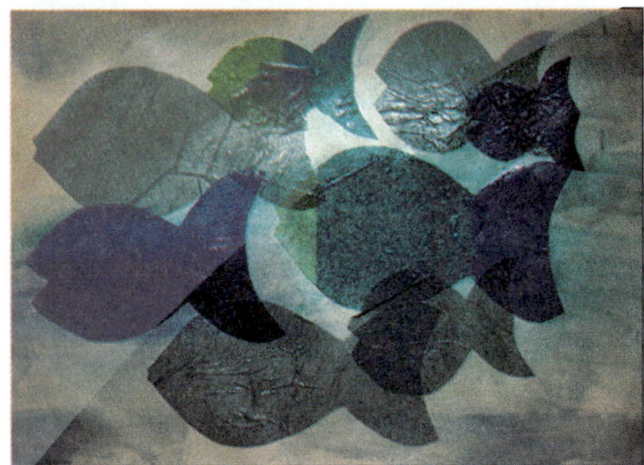

Plate 47. Tissue paper collage

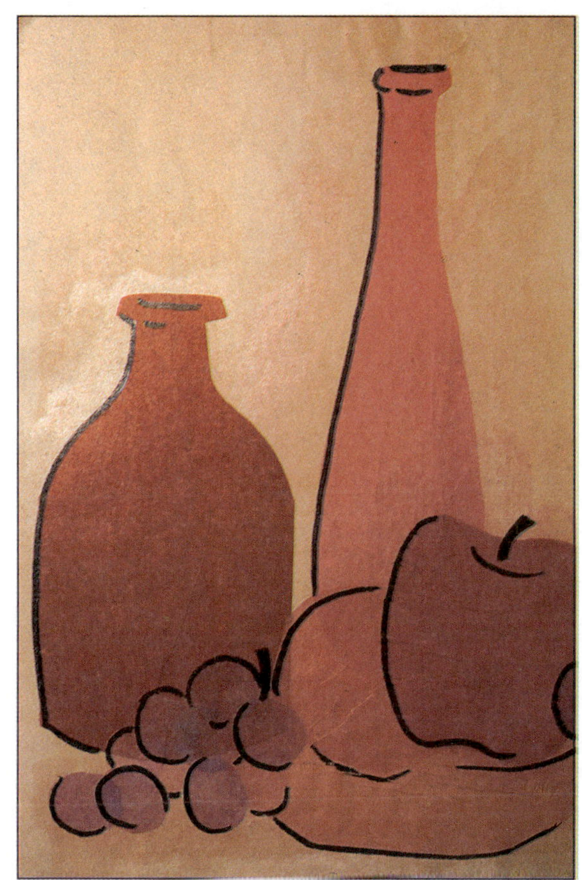

Plate 48. Tissue paper collage

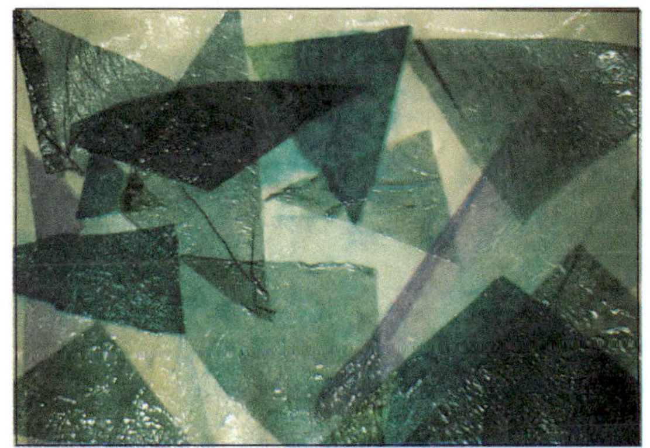

Plate 49. Tissue paper collage

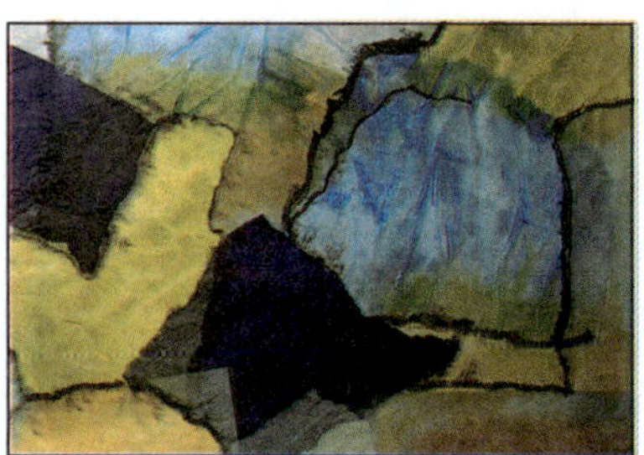

Plate 51. Tissue paper collage

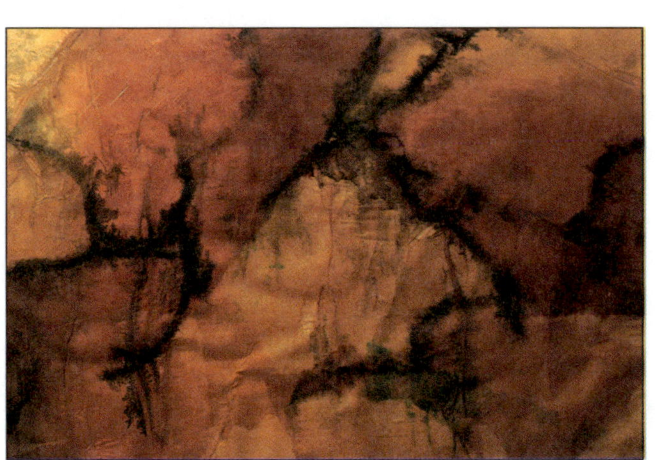

Plate 50. Tissue paper collage

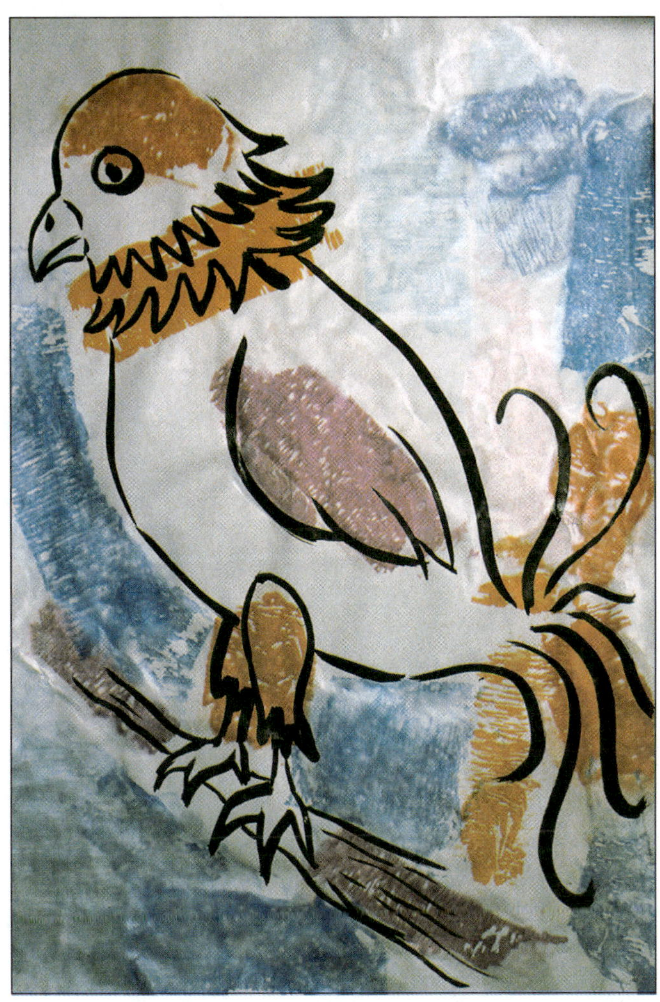

Plate 52. Crepe paper prints

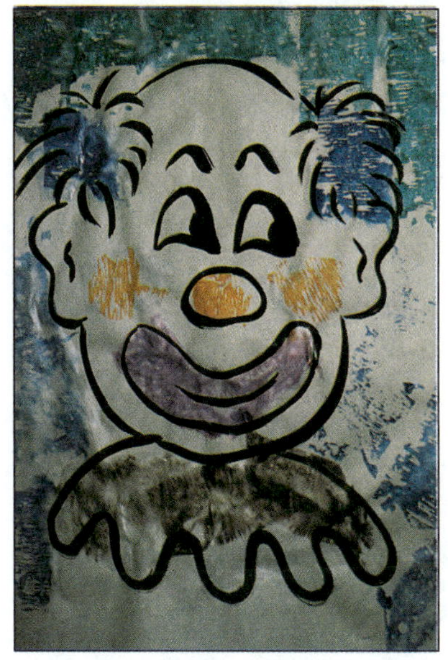

Plate 53. Crepe paper prints

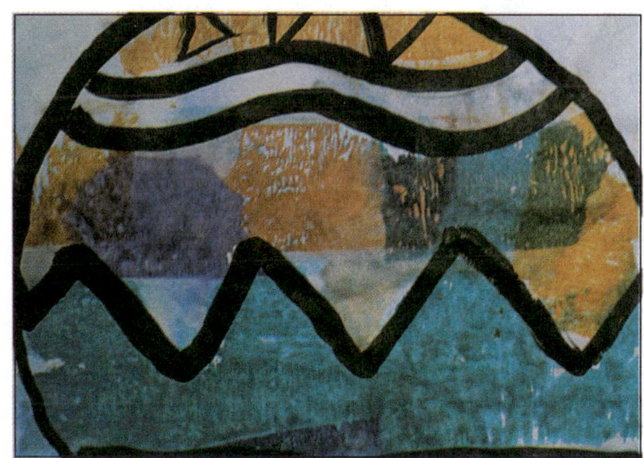

Plate 54. Crepe paper prints

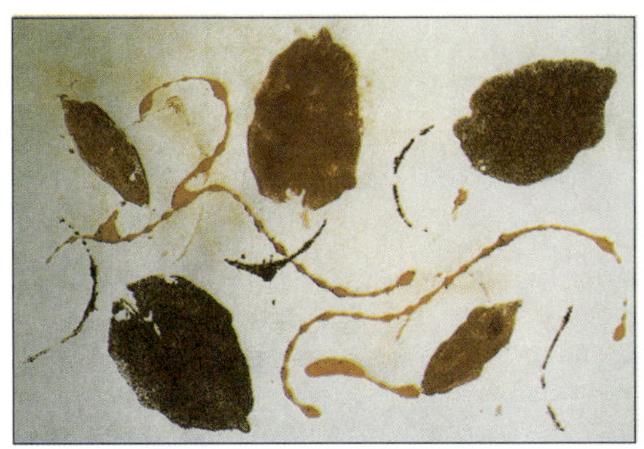

Plate 55. Kitchen powder prints

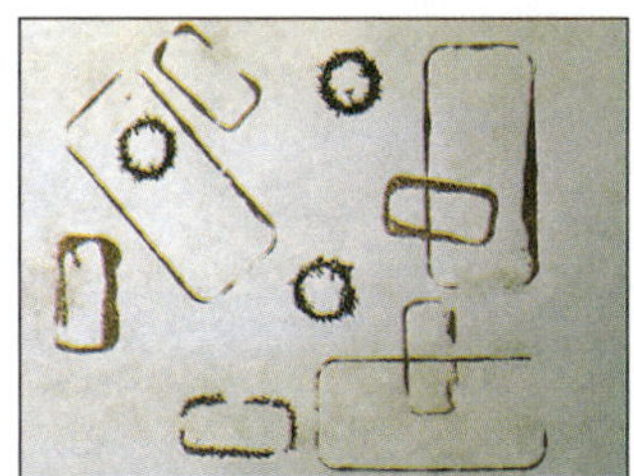

Plate 56. Kitchen powder prints

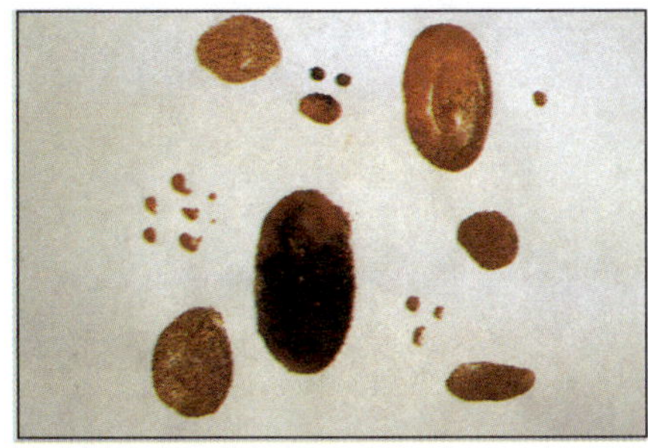

Plate 57. Kitchen powder prints

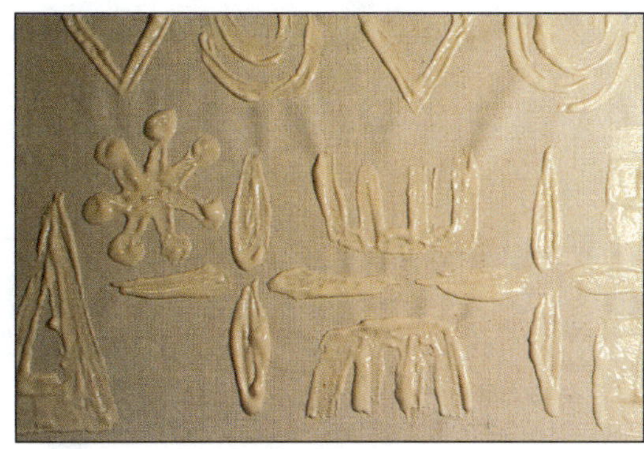

Plate 58. Paste batik unfinished, before adding color

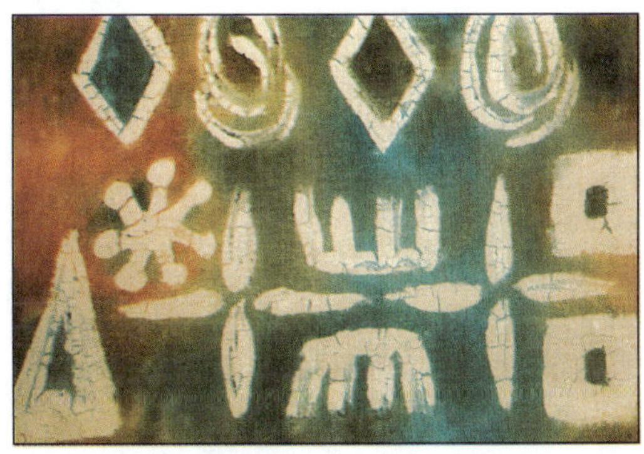

Plate 59. Completed paste batik

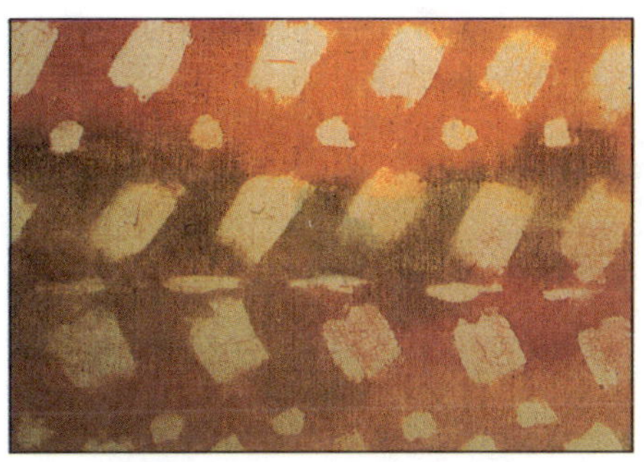

Plate 60. Completed paste batik

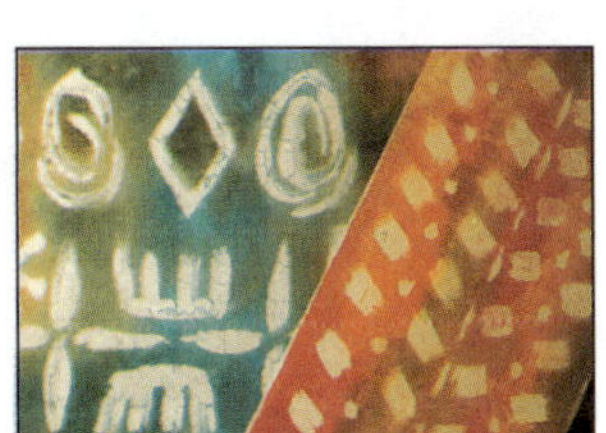

Plate 61. Completed paste batik

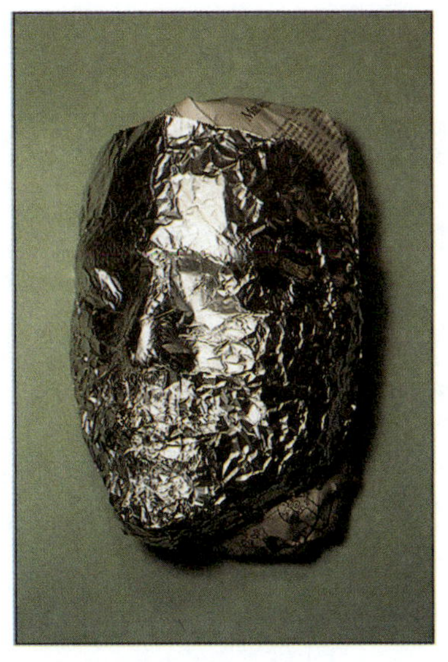

Plate 62. Foil mask on a crumpled newpaper form

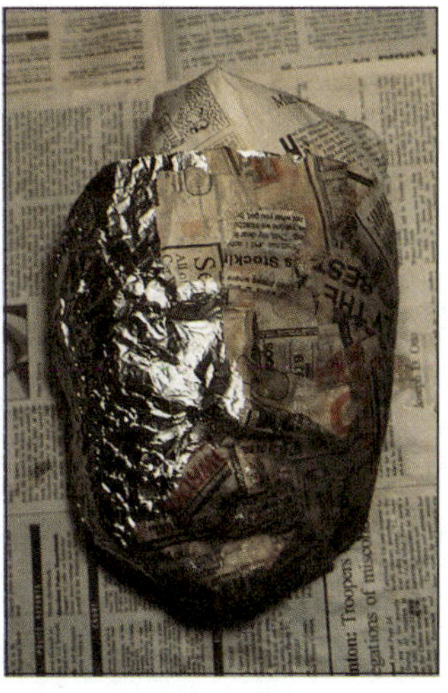

Plate 63. Foil mask half covered in papier-mâché

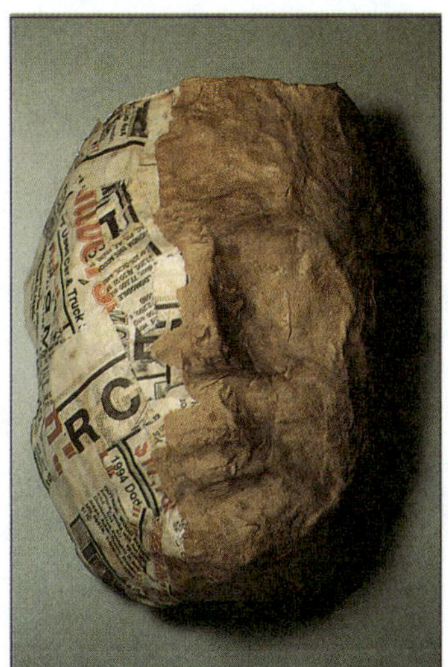

Plate 64. Papier-mâché mask half covered in final layer

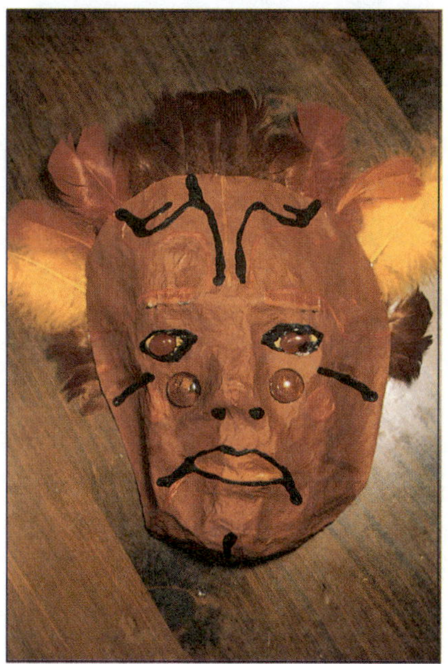

Plate 65. A completed, painted, and decorated mask

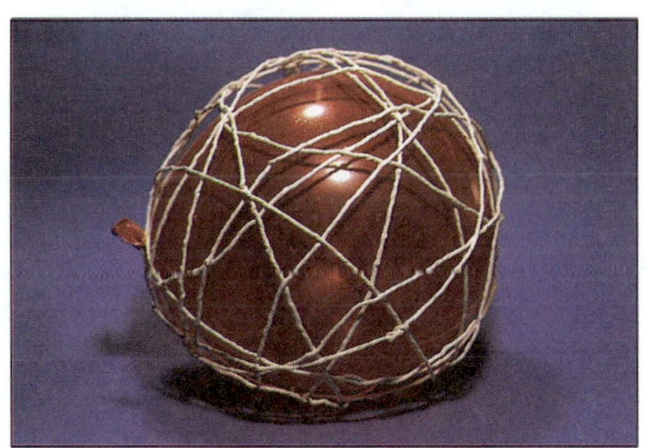

Plate 66. String thing on a balloon

Plate 67. Yarn art with tissue paper

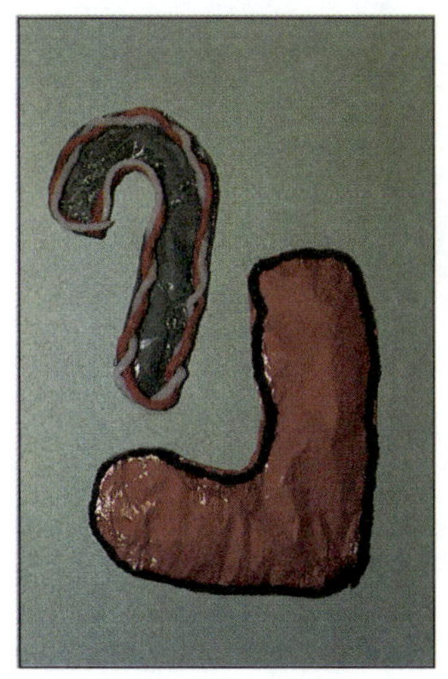

Plate 68. Yarn art with tissue paper

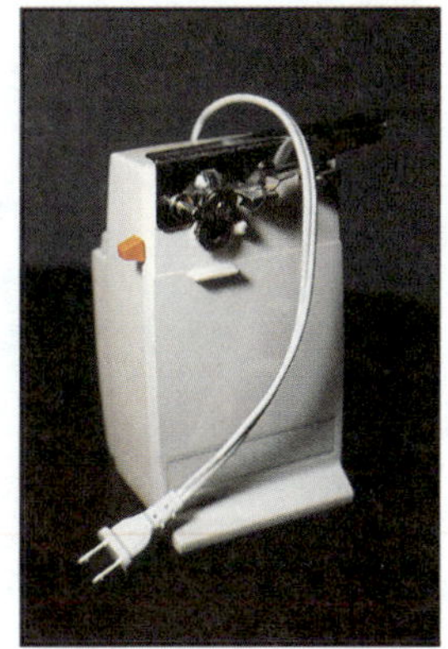

Plate 69. Discarded appliance from this . . .

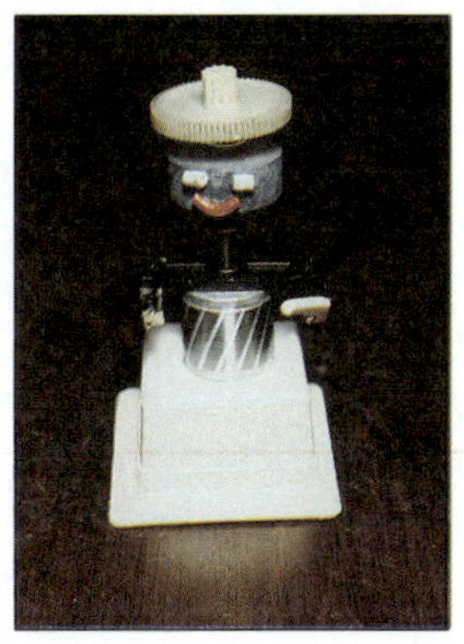

Plate 70. transformed . . .

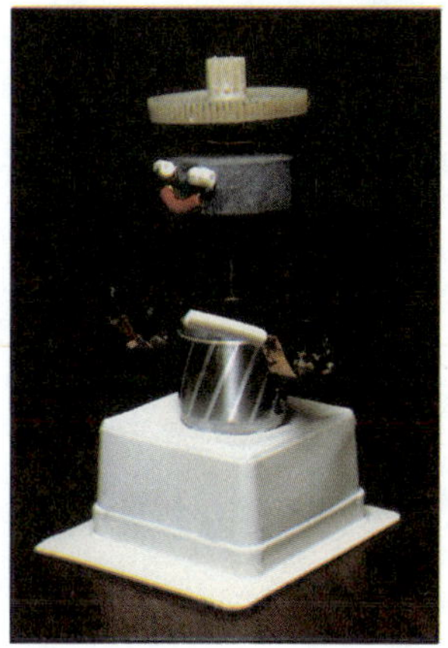

Plate 71. . . . to this.

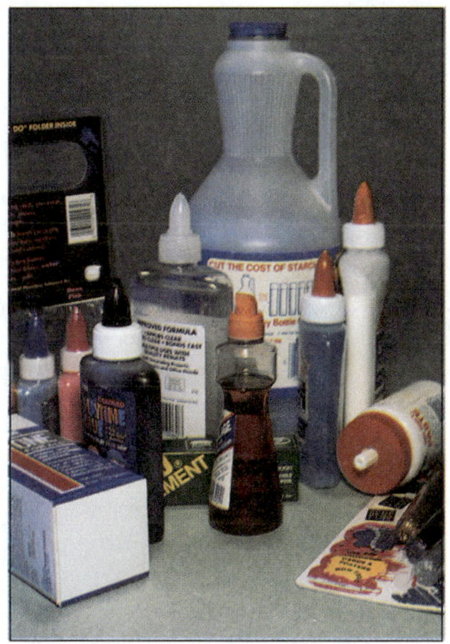

Plate 72. Adhesive products

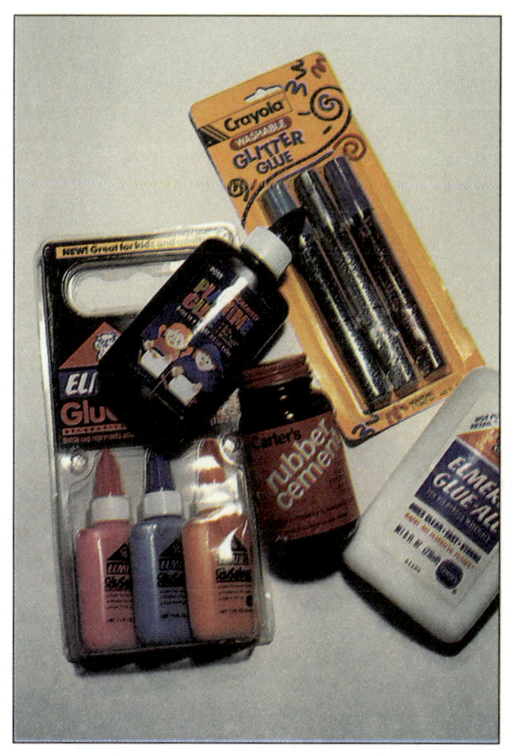

Plate 73. Adhesive products

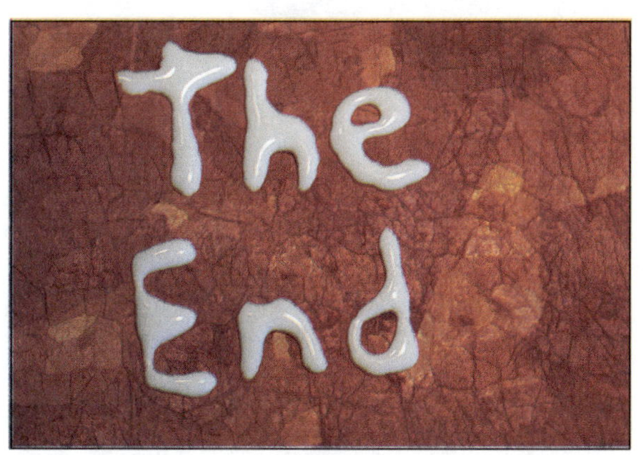

Plate 74. The End

Chapter VIII

Recipes for Fun—Powder Prints, Paste Batik, and More

• Kitchen Powder Prints •

(Plates 55–57)

Skills rating: Easy

Powder prints from the kitchen are colorful (done in gorgeous greens, golds, and rusts) and they smell good too.

You'll need paper, glue, and a variety of powdered spices such as cinnamon, thyme, mace, paprika, ground mustard, oregano, cloves, curry powder, cocoa, red pepper, and chili powder.

You'll also need cut-out cardboard shapes or objects to stamp with, such as leaves or cookie cutters. You'll use these objects to print glue shapes onto your paper. Either paint one side of your object with glue, or press it into a puddle of glue on a piece of scrap paper. When you have coated one side of your shape with glue, press it down onto the paper you wish to print. Lift up the object and quickly sprinkle powder onto the paper. Tip the paper and shake off the excess powder. Collect the excess on another piece of paper if you wish to reuse it.

Print one area of glue at a time, and cover it with powder before going on to more glue shapes.

Variation: Sand Painting

You can create brightly colored sand by crushing colored chalk and mixing it with sand. Sand paintings are done in the same manner as kitchen powder prints: one area at a time.

• Paste Batik •

(PLATES 58–61)

Skills rating: Moderate

Traditionally, batik is a wax-resistant technique for decorating cloth. A wax design protects parts of the fabric when the cloth is dipped in a dye bath. A characteristic of batik is a cobweb effect caused by color flowing into cracks in the wax.

Paste batik, on the other hand, is a starch-resist method. It is related to both Japanese and African dye processes. In the latter, *adire eleko*, Africans use a starch called *lafun* made from cassava flour.

After the fabric has dried following the dye process, the starch is flaked off. Starch-resist designs appear on only one side of the cloth.

You can create batik wall hangings, table runners, mantle cloths, or even fabric bookmarks with this terrific technique. To begin, you'll need some inexpensive cotton muslin (bleached or unbleached), direct from the fabric store. Don't launder it before using. Tape a piece of the muslin, 9 × 12 or larger, to heavy cardboard. Attach masking tape to all four sides of the fabric.

You may double or quadruple this recipe for the paste.

Mix together in a container:

- $\frac{1}{4}$ cup flour
- $\frac{1}{4}$ cup water
- 1 teaspoon alum (from the grocery-store spice section)

Use a stiff brush to apply the paste freehand to the fabric surface. Your patterns may be abstract, nonobjective, or pictorial. Some African designs represent implements such as knives, combs, and mirrors.

Another method of application is to cut stencils from tagboard and force the paste through the openings onto the cloth. Whether hand painted or stenciled, the starch designs must be set aside to dry overnight.

Next, color is applied to the cloth with large brushes. Use either intense watercolors or food coloring mixed with a little water. Colors should be vivid and strong because they'll dry a bit lighter. Some of the traditional African dye colors are indigo blue, black, brown, red, and yellow.

Paint over the entire cloth, designs and all. For that desirable crazed batik effect, press down on the paste shapes and lines as you paint. The dried paste will crack in several places and allow color to seep into the crevices, adding interest.

After the cloth has dried thoroughly, chip off the paste to reveal the white lines and shapes of your pattern. Flake off the dried paste with your fingernails or with a blunt knife. Be patient. Use some of that elbow grease mentioned in Chapter V. When the cloth feels smooth all over, you're done.

The finished fabric can be pressed with a warm iron if necessary. It is not washable because of the water-based colorants.

An ancient art, a captivating craft—beautiful batik is to "dye" for.

Evaluation

Have you varied size, shape, and/or direction in your paste design? Do your fabric colors provide good contrast with the fabric after the dried paste has been removed?

Recipes for Sticky Stuff

Cooked Flour Paste

1 cup flour	3 cups boiling water
1 cup cool water	1 teaspoon alum

Mix the flour and the cup of cool water to a smooth paste. Add 3 cups of boiling water and cook until thick. Add the alum to preserve the mixture and 5 drops of oil of wintergreen, if desired.

Hobby Craft Paste

$\frac{1}{2}$ cup cornstarch	2 tablespoons corn syrup
$1\frac{1}{2}$ cups water	1 teaspoon vinegar

Mix half the cornstarch, $\frac{1}{4}$ cup, with $\frac{3}{4}$ cup water and 2 tablespoons of corn syrup in a medium-sized saucepan. Add 1 teaspoon vinegar. Cook over medium heat, stirring constantly. Stir another $\frac{1}{4}$ cup cornstarch into another $\frac{3}{4}$ cup water until smooth, and immediately stir a little at a time into the thickened mixture. Stir until smooth. If desired, add a bit of oil of wintergreen to sweeten and preserve the mixture. Thickens upon cooling.

Holiday Window Paint

Add 4 tablespoons of mucilage to 1 pint of liquid tempera paint when decorating Halloween or Christmas windows.

This adds enough binder to the paint to help it stick well on glass.

Homemade Finger Paint

6 cups cold water	$1\frac{1}{2}$ cups wheat paste powder
$\frac{1}{2}$ cup powdered laundry detergent	
oil of wintergreen	powdered tempera paint

Pour the wheat paste powder into the cold water very slowly while mixing well. Add the laundry powder and dry tempera and mix well. Makes a large quantity. Wintergreen oil helps to preserve this finger paint.

Carving Mixture

2 cups sawdust	$\frac{1}{2}$ cup wheat paste powder
1 cup plaster of paris	2 cups cold water

Mix together all the ingredients and quickly pour into a form such as a milk carton. Allow to dry. Later cut away the carton before beginning to carve. This is a soft carving material and easy to work with.

Glurch

$\frac{1}{2}$ cup white glue	$\frac{1}{4}$ cup liquid starch
container	newspapers

Stir the two ingredients together in the container, and then knead until smooth. The mixture won't stick to your hands unless you've used too much glue. If it does become too sticky, add 1 teaspoon of starch. If it's too stringy, add $\frac{1}{2}$ teaspoon of glue.

Glurch is fun to handle—shape it, squeeze it, roll it, bounce it. To save cleanup time, work on newspapers when making glurch. You can store glurch in a tightly sealed plastic bag for about a week. When it liquefies, discard.

Papier-Mâché Clay

$\frac{1}{2}$ bucket water	wheat paste
newspapers	oil of wintergreen

Recycle old newspapers into a money-saving compound. Tear them into 1-inch squares and soak them overnight in water. Then pour off much of the water and use an electric mixer to beat the bits to a pulp. Squeeze out the excess water. Add wheat paste (from a wallpaper store) and beat some more, until you have a thick, smooth mixture. Add a few drops of oil of wintergreen, if desired, to help preserve the compound.

When molded into pottery, jewelry, or small sculpture, the clay will take three to five days to dry. It can then be sanded, painted, and sealed.

Papier-Mâché Paste

1 cup flour	2 cups boiling water
2 teaspoons liquid glue	

This is a good substitute for wallpaper paste. Make a creamy paste with the flour and a little cold water. Then add the boiling water and the glue. Mix well.

Sawdust Clay

sawdust	sieve or screen
wheat paste	container
water	measuring cup

Strain the sawdust through the sieve or screen to obtain the finest sawdust possible. Mix 3 parts fine sawdust to 1 part wheat paste in a container, and add just enough water to make a thick, gooey mass. Squeeze and knead the mixture with your hands.

When you're ready to shape the dough into a sculpture, avoid creating anything too large. If the object you model is too fat, the piece may crack when it dries.

This clay smells wonderfully woody and dries to a nice blond color. It has a rough texture which might be very interesting if left that way (but you can sand your sculpture smooth if you wish).

Chapter IX

Marvelous Masks

• Perfect for Partners •

(PLATES 62–65)

Skills rating: Moderate to advanced
Artful recycling

Papier-mâché is not only a great way to reuse newspapers but also an enjoyable art medium. Mâché masks are exciting anytime, but especially when done in this way—up close and personal.

First, you'll need heavy-duty aluminum foil, newspapers, wheat paste or wallpaper adhesive, a container, and white or brown paper towels.

To begin, pair up with a pal if possible. A partner can place the heavy foil over your face and form it carefully to your contours. (Lightweight foil won't keep the forms; it will crumple too easily later.)

When all your facial features have been shaped into the foil, cut the excess from around the edges and place the form on a wadded-up newspaper support.With this prop under the foil face, you'll be able to proceed.

Tear newspaper into strips, going with the grain. Try both directions, and the one that tears straight and long is the one you want. Now tear the strips into pieces no longer than 3 inches.

Next, soak the small newspaper pieces in wallpaper paste and smooth them onto the foil form. Be careful to press only lightly, to retain the foil contours. Mold the pieces around the face properly—the original features will be lost if the newspaper pieces are too large or carelessly applied. When you've finished one layer, do another in a different direction. This adds strength and helps you to remember how many layers you've applied. Another way to keep track of layers is to alternate colored comics with uncolored newspaper pieces. Apply four layers in all.

Then smooth on the final layer: small torn pieces of pasty paper towels. Use pieces no larger than 1 × 2 inches, for the last coat must be as wrinkle-free as possible. Allow the project to dry thoroughly over several days.

Finally, paint the dried mask with acrylics or tempera. If you use the latter, you can add protection and shine with a final coat of clear acrylic spray. You might then try a glitter-glue stick or try trailing colored glue lines in patterns, following the masks' contours. Complete decoration by gluing on buttons, beads, sequins, braid, ribbon, yarn, or feathers.

Is your mask meant to be displayed on a wall as decoration, or is it to be worn? Eyeholes and mouth openings can be cut; tie-ons or a holding stick can attached for actual use.

Mask-making is as old as humankind. Some of the earliest masks may have been used as an aid during the hunt. Other purposes for masks include hiding one's identity, decorating or protecting the face, frightening others, and enhancing rituals.

A mask is almost magical in its ability to transform the wearer. A mask can hide your identity and allow you to acquire a new one. So let's make marvelous masks and try on a new personality.

Evaluation

Is your mask well-crafted, with smooth, well-formed features? Is it sturdy and strong, with about five layers? Do the colors match the mood you're trying to express? Is the surface design appropriate to that mood?

Chapter X

String Things and Yarn Art

• String Things—Perfect for Partners •

(PLATE 66)

Skills rating: Easy to moderate

Make a moonscape or a constellation of heavenly bodies, using balloons, string, and white glue or liquid starch. Newspapers should cover the work surface when you build one of these lunarlike sculptures.

Blow up a round balloon (about 9 inches) and tie it. Fill a shallow container with white glue, which you've thinned with a small amount of water. Liquid starch may be substituted for the glue mixture. Powdered tempera may be added for color.

Soak long pieces of string in the adhesive, and remove excess by pulling the string between your thumb and forefinger. Then wrap the strings firmly around the balloon. Another pair of hands would be very helpful to hold the balloon and to help wrap the string, but an artist working alone can be very successful too. Tuck string ends around and under other strings.

After the balloon is thoroughly covered with a crisscross string thing, allow the sculpture to dry for a few days. Then pop the balloon with a pin, and very carefully remove the pieces of broken balloon between the strings.

These great globes can be suspended with thread from the ceiling for a stellar show. White's nice, but if you prefer colorful spheres, add tempera to the glue before immersing the string. As an alternative, spray paint completed string things after they dry.

With a group of marvelous moonscapes you can present a mysterious spectacle: Create a space mural, hang the sculptures in front of it from the ceiling, turn off the room lights, and aim flashlights at the spheres. Splendid!

• Yarn Art •

(Plates 67–68)

Skills rating: Easy to moderate

Create a "stained glass" mobile or designs to hang in front of a window. Seasonal shapes might become Christmas tree ornaments or package decorations.

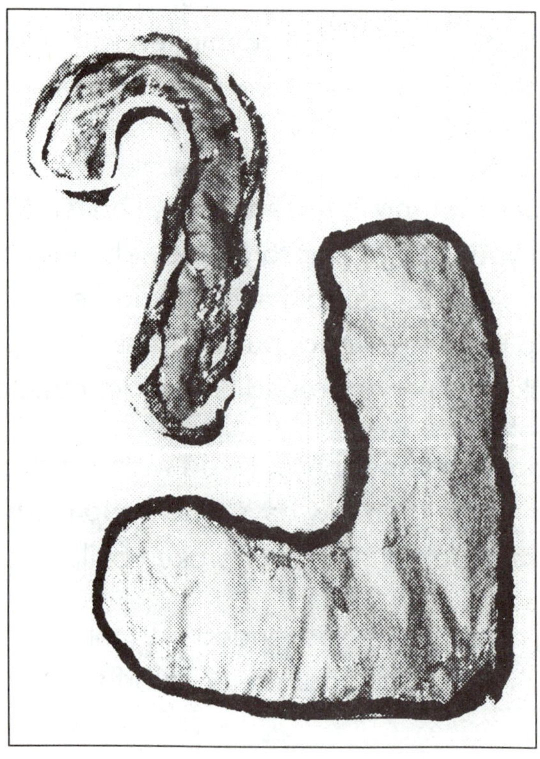

Holiday yarn art with tissue

You'll need brightly colored yarn, tissue paper, waxed paper, white glue mixed equally with water, and scissors.

Place a sheet of colored tissue paper on top of a piece of waxed paper. Soak several lengths of yarn (about 12 inches each) in the glue mixture. Press the yarn pieces into the tissue in the desired arrangement. The glue will soak through the tissue onto the waxed paper beneath, so be sure to peel your yarn-tissue design off the waxed paper before it is thoroughly dry. Move the work in progress to another nonstick area on the waxed paper.

Allow to dry overnight. Then trim the tissue from the edges and add thread with which to hang the yarn art.

These stained glass beauties can be simple or elaborate. You might try twisting or braiding the yarn before soaking it in glue, or try adding yarn details inside the outlined shape.

This is one colorful craft that's fast too. You can easily finish in two 20-minute sessions.

Chapter XI

Made Anew with Glue—Terrific Transformations

(Plates 69–73)

Skills rating: Moderate to advanced
Artful recycling

How many times do you have the fun of actually "deconstructing" something? Disassembling is delightful! And a pile of parts and pieces can rise again as a brand-new construction. Best of all, you're recycling.

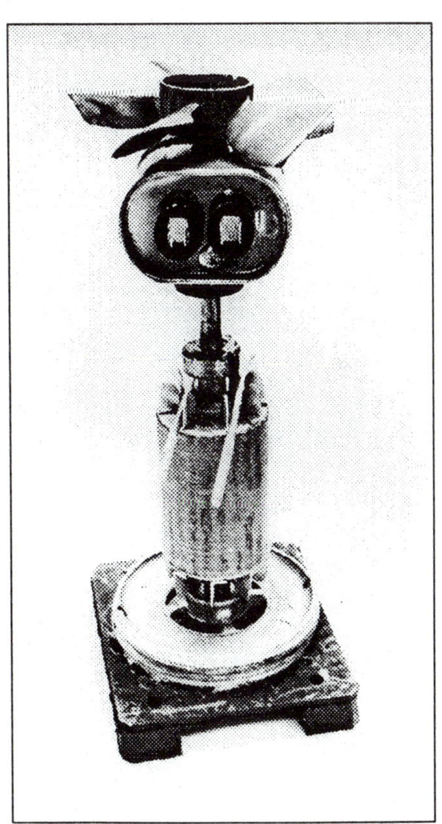

"Robot" made from scrap parts

First, find an old, broken mechanical object: a clock, a toy, a radio, or a kitchen appliance that was to be discarded, for example. Use pliers and screwdrivers to take it apart. Don't be overenthusiastic in your dismantling, and please be careful with small and sharp pieces.

Next, reassemble the parts into a fresh, newfangled form. Try to disguise the object's former condition entirely. If other artists are making objects anew too, you may wish to exchange pieces with them.

Use contact cement or a hot-glue gun to construct your sculpture. If you're using household cement, try clothespins as temporary clamps to hold pieces together until they set.

Note: Be careful with either method—use caution with hazardous fumes or hot glue.

You might form an awesome assemblage that is a plant, a person, a vehicle, an animal, or even an alien creature. Does your creation have to look like something recognizable? No. Nonobjective sculptures are great too.

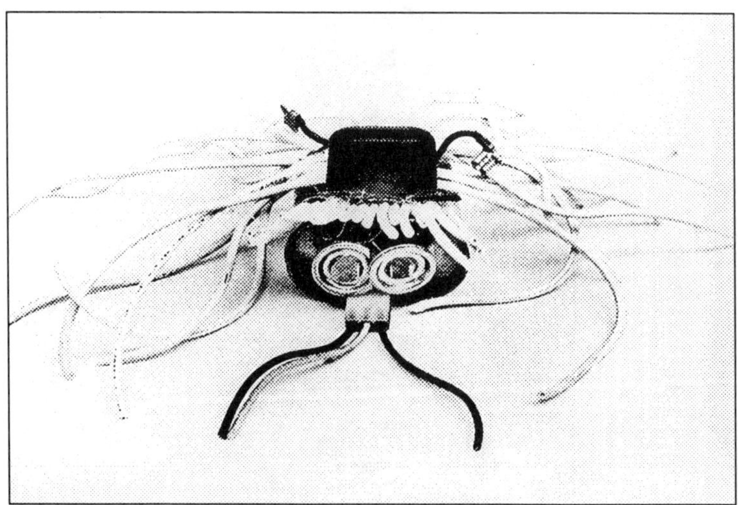

Creature made from scrap parts

Your artwork can be spray-painted when done, to change it even more.

Ready to make thrifty three-dimensional art from throwaways? Let's start transforming!

Evaluation

Is your idea inventive, original, and even ingenious? Is the form interesting from all sides? Is it well crafted and sturdy?

Conclusion

(Plate 74)

Good gracious, what glue can do! You've seen the amazing things adhesives can help you to originate, from light catchers and bird pretzels to yarn and tissue art. We used the resist technique with pastels, watercolor, rubber cement, turpentine, and batik. We printed four different ways. We learned how to transform string, old newspapers, and other discards into delightful three-dimensional artworks.

Modern technology is developing new art products all the time. Use these new materials to make discoveries of your own. Enhance the ideas you've found in this book. The possibilities are limitless. Ideally, you've been inspired to expand your creative skills.

Go ahead, use some great, glorious glue!

GLOSSARY

Abstract—Simplified to the basics.

Accent—A specific area given greater emphasis.

Batik—A method of dyeing designs into fabric by coating with a resist material the parts not to be colored.

Center of interest—That part of an artwork which the artist wishes to express most forcefully; that part which is the first to attract attention.

Clarity—Sharpness, distinctness, definition.

Collage—Method of pasting various materials into visually pleasing form.

Composition—Arrangement, organization of parts into a whole.

Contrast—To show a noticeable difference when compared side by side.

Craftsmanship—Mastery, skill, finesse.

Fixative—Usually a spray, it helps to make permanent such media as charcoal and pastels.

Fluidity—Seeming to flow smoothly.

Focal point—A spot of interest where the viewer's eye is drawn.

Geometric—Square, circular, triangular, etc.; regular.

Intermediate colors—Red-orange, red-violet, blue-violet, blue-green, yellow-green, yellow-orange; the six combination-colors made by mixing a pair of related primary and secondary colors.

Mixed-media—More than one art material, used together.

Mobile—A hanging three-dimensional design with moving parts.

Negative space—The background within which a design is placed.

Nonobjective—Pure design with no relation to natural objects.

Organic—From nature.

Printmaking—Impressing a copy or copies of an image from a master surface; transferring an original as many times as desired.

Pattern—A group of recurring lines, shapes, or textures.

Relief—Where patterns project above a background surface.

Representational—Pictorial; a likeness from life.

Resist—Substance used to cover or protect areas from the application of color (or from the removal of color).

Secondary colors—Orange, green, and violet; made by mixing two primaries together; red and yellow make orange, blue and yellow make green, and violet is made by mixing red and blue.

Tactile—Refers to the sense of touch; see texture.

Texture—Surface quality; how a surface appears or how it feels.

Translucent—Permitting light to pass through.

Unity—Wholeness, undividedness.

Value—Lightness or darkness of a color.

Wash—A thin coat of watery color.